S/4.

GEN
POM

ORIGINAL PRINTS II

New Writing from Scottish Women

Introduction by Elspeth Davie

POLYGON
Edinburgh

First published in Great Britain in 1987
by Polygon Books, Edinburgh.

© Copyright Individual Contributors
Introduction © Copyright Elspeth Davie

ISBN 0 9048275 30 8

Typeset in Garamond by
Edinburgh University Student Publications Board,
48 Pleasance, Edinburgh, EH8 9TJ.

Printed by Biddles Ltd., Guildford, Surrey.

EDITORS' NOTE

Julie Milton, the editor of the first volume of *Original Prints*, wrote that she hoped its publication would give positive encouragement to new women writers.

The reaction from readers, as well as contributors, was such that soon after its appearance we began to solicit material for a second volume. Posters, adverts and letters to writers' groups produced an overwhelming response, displaying both the strength and diversity of women's writing in Scotland. This time we felt that we would more fully represent this variety by including poetry as well as short stories; there is also a piece of non-fiction, further widening the range of writing within.

Another difference of this volume is that far more women were involved in the process of reading and selecting material from the great mass of contributions which descended upon us. We were very fortunate to be working with a number of enthusiastic women who were prepared to devote considerable time and energy to this project. Special thanks are due to Kirsty Reid and Miranda France. All our readers were encouraged by the quality of the work we received and we would extend our thanks to everyone who supported this book by submitting material.

We look forward to the time when it is no longer necessary to strive to balance the under-representation of women's writing. In the meantime we welcome your contributions for the next volume of *Original Prints*.

KASIA BODDY
JANE SILLARS

CONTENTS

Elspeth Davie

INTRODUCTION

The first question is not how well any writing is representative of women or men, young or old, Scottish, English or Japanese, but simply — is it *good* writing? I was thinking of writing a rather general statement about this book, but I know now this would have been very hard to do. The work here is varied and — I have to say it — also very mixed in quality. The best of it is varied, however, in the way people's lives are varied. It is different now with men and women. Not so long ago men hoped to have one, steady job on which their whole day, and often their talk — usually with other men — was centred. Today, a widespread unemployment has changed everything. Men are, unwillingly — to put it mildly — around their own neighbourhood, their own houses and their own women a good deal of the time. For better or worse men and women are close enough to look at one another more keenly, critically. Some of the best writing here comes from the sharp, critical glances of women at men. I daresay an excellent book could be made of the critical glances of men at women — with footnotes thrown in for fun — but somehow there's not so much need for it, as men down the ages have had lots of chances to write such books, or should one say, in fairness, they have made and *taken* their chances.

My hopes for all writing — whether poem, short story or imaginative piece, is that it should be both clever and moving. Some of these pieces I found clever but not moving, and some moving but without the sharpness that makes emotion interesting. Short, pared poems sometimes say more than longer ones. I thought 'Ultra Sonic Scan' was a good example of this. 'Over My Head', 'Ducks', 'Dashed Hopes' and 'Resting' are all short, neat and exact, visually and emotionally. Also the spare, ironic 'For Maria Sibilla Merian' who, in her book, painted a spider eating a bird — and was not believed until the revelation:

> Then, shocked at the unexpected way
> in which gentle nature had
> revealed herself, men ate their words.

'Five Cynical Songs' were all apt and sharp, as is 'Sales Patter', with its resistance to the heart being used as a cheap, breakable, replaceable gadget. There are some very moving poems, — one on hunger, the end of which I quote:

> So they linger,
> the ugly, unlovable glut of dull-eyed waifs
> clutching the filthy hem of the world's skirt.
>
> They sleep a lot: their dreams are crammed
> with sides of beef, mountains of rice.

Moving also is 'Journey near the Border. Poland.' which looks back to Treblinka. 'A Flower for Winter' has a strange, chilly mixture of disappointment and hope.

There are good pieces on love and friendship between women, but to add a welcome, peppery dash of satire in all this comes a funny piece, 'Romantic Friendship and the Modernist Chasm':

> Together they walked by the river holding hands and talking to each other. "Bronwyn," said Bronwyn, "means 'white-breasted', you know." They passed some trees with hanging leaves. "I do love trees, especially when they are so green," said Esther. "Yes," said Bronwyn, "but I like the autumn too."

I must admit I have rather a leaning towards funny stories in these grim times. The transvestite 'An Alternative Romance' was very well done with a splendidly unromantic "happy ending". 'Was Your Mother's Name Jocasta?' should ring a bell with all declaiming writers and those who sit under them. 'Ear-Piercing Screams' and 'The Time My Friend Mabel Became an Anchorite' both bowl along at a comic, confident pace. In fact this book is good on the satire, and I think experience shows that Scottish women, talking to one another, away from the men, have always had a strong line in both satire and ribaldry — far from romantic. And I would say that any attempt to leave women out of things develops this talent for mockery to a very high degree. Being left out sharpens the wits, the eyes and the ears, and to be distanced often means to remain cool and clear. Anyway, Scottish literature is the better for its satire as a safeguard against ever returning to an earlier sentimentality.

Women are supposed to be realists, and I believe it. There has been so much written in the past, for instance, on the glories of pregnancy and the joyfulness of having lots of babies that it really does take a woman to show what it means to be often dead tired from morning till night and to be always vainly hungering for sleep, about which one of the writers in *Original Prints I* has written so well. I must say it used to occasionally cross my mind to wonder why it was the enclosed orders got such cachet for rising at odd times in the night when, for generations, all over the world, women (and men too) have had to get up to attend to small, crying children. Nuns and monks can't help very foolish things being said about them, of course, and they certainly can't help being taken up by cinema. But, let's face it, they do make better film-material than parents in crumpled pyjamas, slippers on wrong feet, wearily crawling away from bed in the small hours — and no melodious bell to help them either. With any luck, though, the young fathers of today usually take a much greater share in responsibility. In earlier days in Ireland, for instance, I remember a man wouldn't be seen dead pushing a pram unless certain he wouldn't be spotted by his mates. Then, while pushing, he would occasionally glance round at the group of older children at his heels to make sure they were all there, though obviously not intending to do any very hard arithmetic on the problem.

Women share guilts and need to express them. There is the guilt of loving their children dearly, but not always feeling absolutely joyful about giving up their independence and their work, about the disturbance to wider outlooks for a while, about new rhythms in marriage and in friendship. Luckily people can talk and write about it now. Good writing is always about these *mixed* feelings. Women somehow are more prone to guilt about them I think, though truly they must know that this mixture has always been the very stuff of an interesting life and of good literature. These feelings have to be sung, howled, chanted, danced, shrieked and expressed in whatever way seems best. Talking of shrieking, I liked the 'Ear-Piercing Screams' mentioned before. It begins in the expectant mothers' class where "pain is taboo". Contractions is the in-word. On the same theme, 'Old Wives Tales'.

'Jamila's Wedding' was, I thought, a beautifully written, sympathetic and finely detailed account of a Moroccan wedding. Two stories, 'Quartet in E Flat' and 'Isle of Man' I found interesting, mysterious and rather difficult with their symbolism of reflections, illusions, loneliness and loss.

Perhaps one day women will feel so much at ease in the world at large and in the literary world that they will feel no special need to write of their own sex or of specifically female things. Like George Eliot they may be able to take everything in their stride, using as their subjects men and women and their work, set against the social and political scene of their own century, finding how it impinges on both sexes. We remember how George Eliot resented being guided, as a matter of course, towards the sofa where the women sat together discussing domestic matters. Certainly the talk there might be different nowadays, but I know that women are still guided gently but firmly towards these sofas. I'm all for comfort and giving the feet a break, but one knows that the 'serious talk' of men for the most part still goes on while they stand up in a closed circle for a very long time, even if the knees buckle at the end of the day. However, men and women talk much more freely together now than in the older generation. Yet Scotland has still a good way to go in this I would say.

It is sad that just when women are supposedly 'free', they find themselves having to be careful in pettier ways than they had bargained for. For instance — not to make too much of a subject we all hear a great deal about — one will not find so many women, young or old, enjoying long solitary walks in lonely places, no matter how independent they are. Dickens, because of his incredibly busy literary and social life, was said to find his freedom to think and observe by taking long walks on his own in the London streets at night. We know there are women who do this, of course, as shown in a fascinating TV documentary of a woman journalist who went out regularly alone at night to find out who the night-workers were, what they did and how they managed to get it done before the morning crowd seethed back to the city. All these jobs were ones the ordinary person knew nothing about.

Women writers may have to cope with a statement I've heard more than once, "But women don't know how to 'do' men — in writing". How odd, since women may live most of their lives with lovers, husbands, fathers, sons, brothers, to say nothing of working alongside men. Strangely enough, you don't hear, "Men don't know how to do women". It's true there are jobs men do that women don't know much about. But they can be told. It is the same with women's jobs. Both can learn from one another. Men and women are different in their sexual acts and feelings. They seldom write easily or adequately about the other's experience in any intimate way. Yet it is the way they come together.

Luckily this book has not too much of the male/female aggression. Conflict, where it comes, is shown in a more subtle way. The aims of this book are not high. Yet, though "soaring ambition" can sometimes be a fine thing — I'd say that, at the start of writing, treading a solid, well-known path isn't a bad thing either — in other words showing honestly how much one knows about what is right under one's own feet.

Finally, I'd like to mention here that there is always work left out of introductions and reviews. It happens to all writers — beginners or 'established' — and is usually because there is a strict word-limit to any article. So it doesn't mean anything then? Oh yes, it does. It means that one must ignore it and go on writing better and more and more confidently.

The sprightly and rather cheeky confidence of this particular volume gives one hope for even better books to come.

Janice Galloway

TWO FRAGMENTS

I remember two things in particular about my father. He had ginger hair and two half fingers on one hand. The ring finger and the middle one fastened off prematurely at the knuckle, like the stumpy tops of two pink pork links, but smoother. They were blown off during the war. This was a dull sort of thing, though; my mother had another story that suited my child-need far better.

It started with the usual, your daddy in the pub. I couldve had a mint of money today if he hadnt been a drinker by the way. Anyway hed been in there all night and he came out the pub for the last bus up the road, but by the time he staggered to the stop he was just in time to see it going away without him. He chased it but it wasnt for stopping. Hed missed it. There was nothing for it but to start walking. He had to go along past Piacentinis on the corner and that was where he smelt the chips. It wasnt all that late yet and they were still open. The smell of the chips was a great thing on a cold night and with all the road still to go up and he just stood there for a wee while soaking up tne warm chips smell. It made him that hungry he thought he had to go in and get some, so he counted all the loose change in his pockets and with still having the bus fare he just had enough. He was that drunk though he dropped all the money and he had to crawl about all over the road to get it all back because he needed every penny to get the chips. That took him a wee while. And by the time he finally got in, Mrs Piacentini was just changing the fat and so he had to wait. That was all right but the smell off the chips was making him hungry by this time. Just when he was about to get served, a big polisman came in and asked for his usual four bags and because he was in a hurry and he was a regular he got served the chips that were for your daddy. So by the time he was watching the salt and vinegar going on to his bag, his mouth was going like a watering can. He was starving. The minute he got out into the street with them, he tore open the bag and started eating them with his fingers, stuffing them into his mouth umpteen at a time and swallowing them too fast. He thought they were the best chips he had ever tasted. He was that

13

carried away eating them that it wasnt til he went to crumple up the empty bag and fling it away he saw the blood. When he looked over his shoulder there was a trail of it all the way up the road from Piacentinis. He was that hungry hed eaten two of his fingers for chips with salt and vinegar.

My granny had a glass eye. She was a fierce woman. A face like a white gingernut biscuit and long, long grey hair. She smoked a clay pipe. And she had this glass eye.

My grandfather was a miner, and the miners got to take the bad coal, the stuff with the impurities the coal board werent allowed to sell. She built up the fire one day and was bashing a big lump of this impure coal with the poker when it exploded and took her eye out.

But my granny was the very stuff of legend so there was another story about that too, centring on other great truths. Again, it was my mothers: I was much too feart for my granny to ask her anything.

Your granny could be awful cruel sometimes. She drowned cats. She drowned the kittens and if the cats got too much she drowned them as well. There was one big tom in particular used to come up the stairs and leave messes in the close. Gad. Right outside your door and everything. Stinking the place out. I dont like tom cats and neither did your granny. She got so fed up with the rotten smell and its messes that one day she decided she was going to get rid of it. So she laid out food and when it came to eat the food she was going to sneak up on it with a big bag. It was that suspicious, watching her the whole time while it was eating: your granny staring at the cat and the cat staring back. It was eating the food in the one corner and your granny was hovering with the bag in the other. High Noon. Anyway, she waited for her minute and she managed to get it. Not right away, though. It saw her and jumped, but it went the wrong way and got itself in a corner and she finally managed to get the bag over it. By the time she got into the kitchen, with the cat struggling in the bag, she was a mass of scratches. The cat was growling through the bag and trying to get its claws through at her again, so she held up the bag and shook it to show it who was the boss. Then she didnt know what to do next, til she clapped eyes on the boiler. A wee, old-fashioned boiler like a cylinder thing on wee legs with a lid at the top. She got a string and tied up the top of the bag and then she dropped the cat right into the boiler drum. It was empty, of course. She was going to keep it in there til the boys came back (thats your uncle Sammy and uncle Alec) and get one of them to take it to the tip and choke it or something. She was fed up with it after all that wrestling about. She got on with her work in the kitchen, and as she was working about she could hear the cat banging about in the boiler the whole time, trying to get out, while she was getting on with the dinner and boiling up kettles of water for the boys coming home for their wash. When they got in from their work, the first thing they did was get a wash: there was no baths in the pit and they never sat down to their tea dirty. Your granny wouldnt let them.

So they came right into the kitchen when they got home and the first thing they noticed was this thumping coming out the boiler. Alec says to her what the hells that mother and she tells them about the tom cat. Just at that the thing starts growling as if its heard them and our Sammy says I hope you dont think Im touching that bloody thing, listen to it. And he starts washing at the sink and laughing like it was nothing to do with him. Even our Alec wouldnt go and lift the lid. So she got quite annoyed and rolled her sleeves up to show them the scratches to tell them she wasnt feart for it and she would do it herself. So after shed gave them their tea, she got them out the kitchen so she could get on with it.

She had thought what she was going to do. First, she got two big stones from the coalhouse and the big coal bucket from the top of the stair. She put the bricks at the boiler side and filled the big bucket with cold water at the sink. The cat had stopped making so much noise by this time so it was probably tired. This would be a good time. She got the washing tongs, the big wooden things for lifting out the hot sheets after theyd been boiled and went over to the boiler, listening. Then she flung back the lid, reached in quick with the tongs and pulled the bag out before the cat knew what was happening. The minute it was out the drum, though, it starts thrashing about again and your granny drops the bag and runs over to the sink for the pail, heaves it over to the boiler and pours the whole lot in. She filled it right up nearly to the top. The bag was scuffling about the floor so she waited til it went still again. Then when it had stopped moving, she gets hold of it with the tongs quick and plonks it straight into the water, banging the lid down shut and the bricks on top.

She went straight into the livingroom to build up the fire and tell the boys shed managed fine without them, quite pleased with herself. She would just leave the cat in the boiler til the next morning to be sure it was drowned and get the bucket men to take it away. Sammy was a bit offended. He said she was a terrible woman but they didnt do anything about the poor bloody cat so they were just as bad. There was no noise in the kitchen when they went in for a wash before they went to their bed. It was a shame.

Well it was still the same thing the next morning when your

granny went in to light the kettle. Nothing coming out the boiler. That was fine. She got me and Tommy away to the school and your uncle Alec and Sammy were away to the pit and our Lizzie was out as well. So that was her by herself and she started getting the place ready for the disposal of the body. She put big sheets of newspaper all round the floor and got the tongs ready. It would be heavy. She shifted one of the bricks off the boiler lid and listened to make sure. Nothing. She shifted the other one off and lifted up the lid. There was a hellish swoosh and the cat burst out the boiler, soaking to the bone, its eyes sticking right out its head. It mustve fought its way out the bag and been swimming in there all night, paddling and keeping just its nose above the water, and the minute it saw the light when your granny lifted the lid, it just threw itself up. It shot out straight at her face and took her eye out just like that. Your granny in one corner of the kitchen, with the eye in another and the tom cat away like buggery down the stairs.

Fingers for the army.

An eye for the coal board.

A song and a dance for the wean.

Rosemary Mackay

A STORY WITHOUT SENSE

Ellen had climbed up behind the corrugated iron sheets stacked in the playground shelter and hidden there, smiling in the near-dark. Though it was the only really good spot left, no one else had dared to go. She crouched and remembered other hiding places, better with a pal, in the woods, ducked down in the broken-off trunk of a tree, crunching wood lice and beetles underfoot, giggling silently.

She could hear the shouts as school mates outran the 'man' to the dell, the slap of feet on concrete as they sped past. And then, the hand-bell clanging to sound the end of lunch break. Ellen crawled backwards out of the small space between sheeting and brick, jumped down and ran squinting into the sunlight. She clapped the 'man' on the back as she passed her:

"Didn't get me," she gasped.

"You were out of the playground. Cheat!" shouted Kath, her sister, catching up and throwing an arm round Ellen's neck. Ellen wriggled free laughing, and jostled Kath into the doorway.

"I'm not a cheat. You're just a useless man."

"Where were you, then?" asked Matty.

"Why? So you can try it next time? Huh! Scaredy-cat." She laughed back at him down the stairs. Then, they were on the landing, and she could see, through the uprights of the banister, the edge of black hem, the two black shoes.

The nun was waiting outside her office, at the top of the stairs, again. Ellen panicked and pushed Matty aside, trying to get back down against the tide of bodies.

"Hey! Watch it!"

She looked down over the heads of children, but too late: the teacher, hand-bell stilled, was on her way up. Someone tugged her arm.

"Hey, Elly, what's the matter?" She was being forced sideways and back, out of the mainstream. Any further and she'd be visible from the head of the stairs. She grasped her sister's hand.

"She's waiting."

"Again! Quick, get behind me, into the wall."

Sucked back in, they climbed. Don't look at her. Just don't let her catch your eye. She won't call. If she doesn't see you, she won't even think of it. Three stairs to go, head down, Ellen stared at the back of her sister's cardigan, a pulled thread with a tuft of wool two-thirds of the way down it. Her mouth was dry, her calf muscles trembling. One, two, three: and light streamed from the open classroom door. She put her head up to gulp air.

"Ellen Fraser!"

Oh God. Oh Jesus, Mary and Joseph.

Ellen's step faltered. Her sister's hand shot behind her back and tugged Ellen's sleeve. She could dare to go on, as though she hadn't heard: but then . . . Her mind closed. She stopped and someone crashed into her, pushing her into the door jamb, as they stumbled past. Ellen began to smile and turned:

"Yes, Mother?"

The thin, white face was tight, framed by an oval wimple. The nun caught the loose edge of her black veil at the neck — *Ellen, your attitude is all wrong* — and with a jerk of the head — *you're not a good influence on others* — flicked the veil back over one shoulder, her mouth pinched in irritation. She gestured Ellen to stand by her side. Unconcerned heads bobbed below and up past Ellen. She was one of them, should be seated by now, getting out her books, calling to her friends. A boy tripped on the edge of the long, tubular screen, school projector next to it, where it lay on the floor by the wall. Help with carrying that. That was all. Ellen shot a glance up at the nun's face, encouraging the words of command:

"Wait at my door," she said, without a downward flicker of her eyes.

Ellen, still smiling, inclined her head, as they had been taught to do at shrines and statues, and turned into the short, dark corridor which was the entrance to the Headmistress's office.

Every day. Every day for a week. And lots of times before that. Standing in there. Being talked at, on and on: words that went round and round. Like scribbles on a page. *Not like the other children. Different. Why are you different, Ellen? I'm trying to understand you.* And the eyes boring into her.

The flow of bodies was becoming a trickle. Ellen stood in the darkness and stared at the place where her feet should be, aware that she was panting. She dragged her palms down her thighs and swallowed hard on the lump in her throat, no spit to gather. After a while, in the office, breathing became difficult. It was a stuffy, horrible room. But she must smile. Whatever was said, she mustn't stop smiling. Sticks and stones . . . The Staff Room door above and beyond the nun's shape opened noisily and a blonde-grey head appeared, in tight curls, wreathed in smoke, closely followed by a large, fat body.

At the sight of her own teacher, Ellen pushed herself off the wall and began to flap her hands at her sides. She craned her neck, poking her face towards the light. She cursed her dark clothes. Even a pair of white socks would have helped. The teacher rumbled down the few steps to the landing, where the nun stood.

"Good afternoon, Mrs Ritchie," the black head nodded sharply.

"Good afternoon, Mother Morran." Mrs Ritchie had stopped to wrestle with a pile of books in her arms. She turned and peered towards Ellen.

"Oh God, please," Ellen shuffled her feet.

Mrs Ritchie walked away, and the nun swooped down to her office.

They stood together in the tiny space, the nun fumbling with a pile of keys at her belted waist, Ellen pressed back against the wall, in dread of the touch of her habit. The door opened, and the nun entered the small, overfurnished room. A skylight on the sloped ceiling spilled a square of sunshine across her desk; the only other window, high up on the outside wall, had frosted glass which broke up the light.

"Come in, Ellen."

Ellen pulled her mouth back into a smile and stepped across the threshold.

"Shut the door." The nun sat and began moving papers around on her desk. Ellen positioned herself opposite. There was nowhere to look except at the nun. She thought of nothing, stiffly waiting. Then, the shuffling of papers stopped. The nun pushed a hand inside her bodice, and produced a large, gent's watch. She flipped the lid, stared for a moment at the watch face, then snapped the lid shut. Ellen's body twitched and the nun looked up quickly into her face. Ellen chose a point four inches above the nun's head and smiled at it.

"Ellen, look at me."

She sat just beyond the shaft of sunlight, momentarily lost to sight, till the stark, white face took shape. She had the palest eyes that Ellen knew of, with tiny, red veins at the extreme edges. Ellen fixed on the bridge of her nose.

"Well then . . ." she suggested.

Ellen shifted onto one foot and locked the hip. Her hands were clasped wetly behind her back and she concentrated on her balance.

She lifted her shoulders in a shrug and smiled, wider. The white face moved, the mouth opened, closed almost soft.

"Just as you wish, Ellen."

The nun scraped her chair back from the desk, the black garments rolled in rigid folds, the veil collapsed sideways in a head tilt. The large, silver cross moved off the nun's flat chest and swung free. An arm flapped out, crooked, a bony white hand curled at the end. Ellen moved her head to see, following the direction of the pointing hand. She turned back to the nun, questioning.

"Round here, Ellen. Come round."

Ellen thought hard about the manoeuvre, giving suddenly onto the other foot and willed her body round and forward, towards the nun. The nun's arm went tight round her waist and Ellen looked quickly into and away from the grey eyes, the nun's breath already enclosing her.

"That's better, isn't it? Close like this?"

Ellen dropped her head, slowly raised it.

"I have a story that I want to tell you."

Ellen watched the dust motes dancing in the sunlight. What fun to stretch and catch them; to search for them in the palm of her hand and throw them, invisible, back into the light.

"A story about a young nun who became a saint."

Ellen turned her eyes to a picture on the opposite wall. Jesus with children, birds wooden on the ground, lambs hewn out of marble: the words at the foot of the picture said, "Suffer the little children to come unto me".

"This young saint was so good, so holy and so young, that not everyone in the Convent liked her. Some of her sisters in Christ were jealous of her goodness, and one of them tried to stop her being good by teasing her all the time."

Ellen slowly gripped her skirt at the thighs and wrung out her hands. Children shouldn't suffer to go to Jesus. Or Jesus shouldn't suffer because of the children. The picture dimmed and shifted. A hard blink brought Jesus' bearded-woman's face clear. Ellen's kneecaps were quivering. She bent one leg and leant out of the nun's embrace. The arm tightened on her waist.

"One day, the jealous sister-nun began to splash water into the saint's face while they were together, washing clothes at a sink. The saint did nothing. She wasn't supposed to speak anyway. A Rule of Silence. Her sister-nun splashed more water. But, for the saint, it was as if it wasn't happening." The nun leant forward, twisting her head to look up into Ellen's face. A musty smell of air-starved clothes rose into Ellen's nostrils. She turned to the red-veined eyes, slowly craning her head back as she did so. The dust particles danced higher, momentarily frenzied, then drifted. Up in the skylight, dead bluebottles dangled. Suffer the little children, suffer the children. Ellen's face ached with her smile, her mind seeming to float inches above her head.

"The saint didn't know why the nun disliked her. So she prayed harder for understanding. She prayed for the nun, and she prayed to God to take her into Heaven."

Jesus, Mary and Joseph, I give you my heart and my soul. Jesus, Mary and Joseph, I place my trust in Thee. Jesus, let me go.

The nun moved her arm suddenly from Ellen's waist, and Ellen staggered backwards two, three steps: stopped. The nun stared at her. Ellen felt hot all over. The sweat broke on her neck, face and backs of knees. She took a hesitant step forward. The grey eyes were hard.

"The saint knew humility. She knew love. And she loved God and goodness more than anything. Ellen, why do you smile all the time?"

Ellen shrugged, shuffled her feet, looked round at the circular, opaque window above her head.

"It's not a nice smile, Ellen. And it doesn't make you look very pretty."

Ellen opened her mouth to speak and the words, sharp and quick for a second, drifted away.

"Yes? Yes! What is it, Ellen?"

"I've forgotten." She smiled easily. It was true. She had nothing to say. The story was finished. A story without sense.

"Forgotten! You expect me to believe that silliness? Forgotten. Well, we'll see." The nun gathered her long skirts in one hand and turned her body away from Ellen's.

"Tell Mrs Ritchie you were with me. Go."

"Thank you, Mother." Ellen curtsied, walked quickly to the door and closed it behind her.

In the dense passage, she dropped her eyes to the darkness at her feet, easing off her neck. She was desperate to go to the toilet, but would have had to ask the nun's permission to go. She walked through the Primary Four and Five classroom and into her own.

"And where this time?" bawled Mrs Ritchie, who was leaning against the only radiator, book in hand.

"With Mother Morran." Ellen didn't look at her, or at her sister's anxious face over in the Primary Seven rows. She sat down and drew her finger along the familiar, etched grooves on her desk-top. She wanted, more than anything, to sleep.

"Oh, very cosy. Just the two of you. Again." Some of the children giggled.

"You come in here, as bold as brass, disrupting my class, ready to make trouble. But I know the weepings and wailings that go on."

Weepings. Crying. Ellen looked round at the faces. They all showed surprise. A few sniggered.

"Not crying. I don't cry. I wouldn't!"

Through her rage, Ellen saw Mrs Ritchie's face change. Something. Some question. Then she realised that she had stood up. She flicked the seat down into a crash and sat. She knew what her sister's face would say, so she stared at the blackboard-shapes.

"Matthew McHugh, go and sit next to her and share your book. Now that she's here, she might as well join in the work of the class."

Ellen put up her hand:

"Please. I need to go to the toilet."

"Well, you've wasted enough of my time already. If you still need by the end of English ask then."

Ellen crossed her legs and turned to Matty. He smelled sour and his teeth were stained. He was the thickest pupil in the class. Ellen moved closer to him and bent her head to his.

Elise McKay

THE AMMONITE

He took the fossil gingerly
and held it in his hand.
It was too hard
for his ten years to comprehend.
I thought he'd ask, how old?
Instead, "What was it like — alive?"
I tell him "It was curled and soft,
could feel, like you."

His hand in answer tightens round the stone
as though he tried to force the meaning through.
No use; his grasp uncurls,
he loses interest, hands it back.
But I have seen the fossil imprint
on his plam. Three million years
to make this one soft mark.

Linda McCann

CROCODILE TEARS

The fixed postures were all very natural.
There was Spider Monkey, swinging along,
And there he was again in just his bones.
Some snakes were woven onto trees, others
Showed that snakes are ladders inside.
Then I saw a miniature crocodile
Houdinied in a sealed jar, half born,
Clawed fists squeezing down to roll away his egg,
Neck stiff in die-hard birth throes; one last pull.
Crumpled armour hanging on heaving bones,
An old man getting out of an armchair.
A prisoner, tunnelled into headquarters.
Behind him, his shadow a pregnant skeleton;
Above him, world-shaped air bubbles.

Helen Lamb

THE WITCH

Leslie Brown is panting and wheezing with excitement. She knows the answer. *Please miss. Please miss. I know.* She would. I hope the fat cow explodes. All round me, frantic fingers are clicking to be picked. But the witch has a long nose. She can smell a slacker a mile off. She ferrets them out with her beady eyes and pokes them with sarcasm till they squirm.

The witch has seen me with my hand down. Her X-ray vision has parted the sea of hands and homed in on me. Her eyes bulge. The eyeballs are a sickly, jaundiced yellow. She wants me to tell her the answer.

But I don't know.

Well, work it out then.

I still don't know.

Make an attempt.

I don't know . . . Um . . . what was the question again.

Wrong, wrong, wrong, wrong and wrong again. "I don't know" is incorrect. Big mistake. The correct answer to the question is "I don't care". Right. V.G. I don't care for your crappy question. Three dots for therefore — therefore I don't care if I'm wrong. Because I like my own questions better than yours anyway.

Take, for instance, the question of the square root of the witch. Now, there's a question. She doesn't have red blood. Her skin's so yellow, the blood is probably all bilious and black. Probably her organs are all black too. Because her blood is like thick, black treacle. So it sticks to her guts. And the black blood shows through the white skin sort of greenish-yellow and makes her look sea-sick and mean.

The witch is watching me. She's got a face like a ferret and thick, black eyebrows that meet in the middle and teeth like the yellowed ivories on an old piano. She's also got a gold filling at the side which you only see when she smiles. And she only ever smiles when she's being sarcastic. Wrong, wrong, wrong — and then, you see the gold filling.

Her eyes are bulging again. Aha — caught one with her hand down. She says she's had enough of my indolence.

wouldn't matter so much if I was blonde. But girls of my age are sensitive. And even Caroline — whose father is Baptist and doesn't have a television — bleaches the hair on her legs. Caroline has shiny, black hair like mine.

Mum didn't want me to come home crying because of Edward and the Fatboy again.

Edward has a suppurating, acne-pitted nose. And the Fatboy's got piggy eyes and green teeth. So why should I care about their comments? We used to make comments all the time. And they stuck chewing gum in my hair and I pulled theirs. It was just a laugh, really. I never mentioned Edward's nose or the Fatboy's teeth. So why did they have to go and make comments about my hairy knees?

Girls aren't supposed to have hairy legs.

I hate them both. I hope the Fatboy gets so fat he'll never be able to sit with his knees together. I hope Edward's nose explodes.

The witch doesn't forget.

As there's no class I've to hand in the extra work first thing in the morning. Tomorrow is the end of winter term. We go to church to sing 'There is a Green Hill far away'. That song is beautiful enough to make me want to weep even though I chew gum and try to act more jaded than anyone.

The witch will be wearing face powder and lipstick. She always does on special occasions, like the end of term assemblies and the senior dance. She paints her mouth true red, like a forties movie star. It doesn't suit her. Her lips are too thin and the colour bleeds grotesquely from the corners of her mouth. I wish she wouldn't try. I wish she would go and wipe it off, this instant!

The witch will look gruesome and happy. She always does at these Events. With the make-up on, her face relaxes. Her everyday maths class face demands respect. But not this ghastly celebration mask. It makes me uncomfortable.

People will be sniggering. Especially those bitch perfectionists like Heather — blonde and voluptuous — Rae. I won't. I don't think it's funny in the least. Nothing to laugh at. I'm embarrassed for her. Not that I actually like her but that cursed face can't be all her own doing.

I wonder what she was like when she was young. Not pretty. But, maybe, quite striking. Her figure's still good. Full busted and slim hipped. I wouldn't mind being that shape. I wonder what she was like when her flesh was fresh and plumped out.

I can see her on an old, black Raleigh cycling to meet her lover. Her dark hair curled and bouncing in the wind. Ivory skinned — I don't think the witch ever had much colour — and blood red lips. Maybe

THE WITCH

Put in brackets — (A for apathy + B for boredom) = C me after class.

So I have to go home and wash my brains out with calculus. The witch says that, sooner or later, I will understand that mathematics trains the mind. She says that, no matter how diabolical the calculation, there is an answer to every problem. And life is a drudgery, young lady.

The witch says if I put my mind to it I could get an A. I don't believe her. I couldn't. My mind refuses to be put to it. As soon as I set foot in her class my mind slips sideways and wanders off. I can feel it sort of lurch sometimes.

She says if I really tried I could do well. I can't argue with her. Arguing with the witch is not done.

Her eyes seem to be a bit watery. And she has a queer, close-lipped smile. I think there's a bit of the witch that hurts easy. But, then again, it could be a head cold. Maybe, she's going to sneeze.

She doesn't.

Well — I have to say I'll try. The trouble with maths is you can't argue with it. It's far too neat and tidy. All these small, orderly steps. Those absolutely perfect answers.

You can't say 99 might make a more interesting answer than 100. You can't say that due to Euclid's limited social environment, he could have been mistaken about the shortest distance between two points. Maybe it's not always a straight line. Maybe — somewhere else — it's curved.

Nobody says how come. Nobody asks questions. Answers only, please. We'd never get anywhere if everything was open to argument.

It's too cut and dried for me. Let the witch be the Keeper of the Perfect Answers. I don't want to be her successor. Anyway, Leslie Brown always knows the answer.

I've to hand in the calculus tomorrow. I think the witch has forgotten there's no class tomorrow.

Hairy legs.

The witch has hairy shins and black, knotted veins on her calfs. I can't understand why she doesn't depilate. What is the point in wearing sheer stockings? The nylon only flattens the hairs and makes them splay and twist. Or they poke through the micromesh. If she was a blonde it wouldn't matter so much.

When I was thirteen, my mother bought me one of those depilatory creams which leaves your legs silky smooth and smells revolting. Gran said she shouldn't pander to my vanity. She says I spend too much time in front of the mirror as it is. Mum said it she plucked her eyebrows then. And dyed her legs with tea leaves. She's wearing a gored, knee-length, tweed skirt and a simple, boxy blouse.

Her lover is home on leave from World War II and this is the last time she'll ever meet him. No, he didn't die in battle. That's too corny. Grief didn't turn her so sour.

No. Maybe, that last night, he gave her a present. A small diamond solitaire which had cost him the best part of three months' pay. She was overjoyed. She couldn't wait for the war to be over. She wrote to him every day.

He also gave her a dose of gonorrhoea which he'd picked up cheap in the desert and she didn't discover till ten months later. She was left infertile and without a good excuse to stop teaching maths to a bunch of snotty kids like me, who hated it.

Or, maybe, it wasn't that at all. Maybe, during the Allied Advance he met a Roman waitress who shaved her legs and didn't know the perfect answer to everything. He brought her back to his home town and they opened an ice cream parlour and had four sons. The witch taught them maths at the local high school and all four of them were hopelessly innumerate but handsome in an Italian waiter sort of way.

The witch doesn't like ice cream.

I could stay home tomorrow. It's the end of term. And the witch might forget about the calculus.

FOUR POEMS

by Angela McSeveney

COLIN

Colin presided at my first tutorial,
read sex into all the symbolism,
told the tutor where to get off.

He wore striped trousers and pied shirts,
spoke of love being made in the room next to his.

To catch his glance made me blush.

We shared classes again in our second last term.
I wore pink dungarees at the front of the class.

Colin sat behind me in a herrng-bone coat
and took Jane Austen very seriously indeed.

BETWEEN FRIENDS

He said it might happen again
but really it was just for the moment
between friends.

We didn't let our other flatmates hear.
At one am we sat still
as someone came home late.

He kissed no further than my breasts
and whispered his fears of losing me
as a friend.

Around three o'clock he threw me gently
from his room.

I washed away the dampness where
my body had waited for his.

Two of us were having breakfast
as he left for work.

Just before the door closed I said
self-consciously 'Take care.'

DASHED HOPES

(to Andrew)

His goodbye hug was the first time
anyone had volunteered
to touch me.

His brown checked shirt smelled of sweat.
He stroked my hair just once.

Shaking like a leaf
I spun out five seconds
to last a lifetime,   if they had to.

It felt as intimate as making love.

A long time later
I cried very hard.

I hadn't known that poems speaking
of a lover's heart-beat
simply state the truth.

ULTRA SONIC SCAN

In a standard issue one size shift
I present myself as a votive offering.

I am laid out
and warm oil poured
across my body.

Cold metal skims along my skin
and makes invisible incisions.

I can't read the omens
as my insides flicker
on a black screen.

Jennifer Russell

I WENT ROUND EUROPE

I went round Europe, not Youth Hostelling though. No, we had those Inter-Rail cards and we, me and my mate, just crashed out on the trains. In Greece you could sleep on the hotel roofs or on the beach — if you were on the beach you just buried your rucksack in the sand and then slept on top of it. All the girls just went topless, on some beaches lots of people were just naked. My tan's not bad, is it? It's been a couple of months now. A lot of people go to those sunbeds to keep their tans, but I can't be bothered with that — it's all really false, isn't it?

Are you on the Pill? I'm just asking because I think it's really bad to pump all those chemicals into your body, right? Everything's just really fake, fake tans, false hair, false fingernails, nothing's left to nature. Oh yeah, about Europe. It was amazing the way we left — we had the tickets and everything, we were just buying the ferry tickets down there. Me and my mates all went out that night and got really drunk and the next morning me and Martin just looked at each other and said "Let's go". So we just went. I threw some stuff into a rucksack and left a note for my sister saying "Gone to Europe" and then we went round to his place to get his stuff and then away.

Europe was really great though. We went through Paris, Madrid, along the south coast of France. In Spain the drink was really cheap, and there were some great bars in some of the big coast towns in France where you could just drink all day and all night if you wanted to — and you could smoke whatever you wanted and nobody gave a damn. We went right down Italy, across to Greece then back up through Rome and Florence, saw all the sights. Then Martin went back down to Greece to look for a job and I headed for Switzerland; I just travelled about where I felt like it and stopped in really out-of-the-way places.

I stayed in a Youth Hostel in Switzerland — they don't like you sleeping rough there. In this place, Rheinfaltx I think it was, they let me stay even though I'm not in the Association — I promised I would join. I remember one night I went down to see the waterfall (there was this waterfall right beside the Youth Hostel). Before I'd only seen it during the day. This night it was floodlit and I stood out on the platform almost underneath it. I'd been on my own for a week or so and I hadn't taken anything, but I can tell you I got the biggest lift I've ever had in my life just looking at that waterfall. It was just so beautiful and so clear. At first I thought it was Switzerland — everything was so fresh — but then I found that France was the same, and London. It was pure somehow.

I know what you think, you look at me and think "He's really out" and you see that look in my eyes, and you wonder what I'm on because you know I must be on something. Well, you're right, but I wasn't on anything then — I was on my own and for the first time in a long time I wasn't taking anything.

Just before I started back for home I got into another Youth Hostel, this time in Paris — it was a real dump. In the morning, though, you got bread and jam and you could have a bowlful of chocolate or coffee. I remember sitting with my bowlful of coffee and looking at it and thinking, "This is a bowl of coffee". It just suddenly hit me that I was sitting with a plastic bowl and in that bowl was hot coffee which I was about to drink. It made me feel really strange. I started to think about my mates, and my sister and her boyfriend, and what we all did at home; and it seemed really stupid — what we did — when I could be sitting with a bowl of coffee. Then I knew I had to get back.

The journey back was shattering, especially the coach ride up from London. I hardly slept at all, all night. It was dawn as we came into Glasgow, and the clouds were beautiful. I looked at them and thought that I wouldn't see them like that again for a long time — I would think that I could see more than they were, or I wouldn't notice them at all.

I'd phoned from London and my sister and her boyfriend were waiting at the terminus, and this is the best bit. I'd been away for weeks and knew that I was back and would see my mates that night, and as we got into the car my sister's boyfriend just said "Welcome home" and pressed this big lump of black into my hand. I can't explain just how I felt, to be back, knowing I'd see my mates and then being handed this black. It was the best bit of the holiday.

Sue Gutteridge

FOR EILEEN

You said
'I like the shape of our friendship'.
True, it had a definite beginning.
The accidental meeting at the formal luncheon
Was instant joyful connection.
We were the last to leave. Drunk at 4 p.m.,
You thanked our host for coming.

But its beginning, like its end, was out of character.
For the most part it was a married female friendship
Conducted Monday to Friday, nine to five.
No all nighters.
No no-holds-barred drunken confidences.
No weekends.
Married female friendship —
An art form, bred of constrictions
Which are the stuff of it.
Fitted in the spaces between the children.
Half sentences thrown across the noise of playing
Or fighting.
Patrick kicked me.
I want the doll's pram.
Clara's cut herself — there's *blood*.
I want a biscuit.
Anyway, it's time to go.
The men are coming home.

Was it death that did it.
Gave the friendship its shape.
Hot-housed it.
Gave it the lovers' mode
Of precious, planned-for time
Stolen from children, men, work.

Long journeys for brief meetings
Rich with significance.
Mutual, pleasurable self-analysis when you said,
'I like the shape of our friendship'.

Alison Smith

ROMANTIC FRIENDSHIP AND THE
MODERNIST CHASM

Esther and Bronwyn met through a friend of a friend of Esther's. Soon they became firm friends; they held many views in common.

Bronwyn met Esther by the flowerstall and together they walked by the river, holding hands and talking to each other. "Bronwyn," said Bronwyn, "means 'white-breasted', you know." They passed some trees with hanging leaves. "I do love trees, especially when they are so green," said Esther. "Yes," said Bronwyn, "but I like the autumn too." Their hands were not in the least bit sweaty. They smiled faintly at American and Japanese tourists on the bridge as they passed.

Bronwyn lit a candle in her room, and the light danced.

Esther was a self-confessed artist.

She told Bronwyn on their first meeting. "I am a self-confessed artist," she said, "I don't mind admitting it. I have never felt myself to be anything but an artist in my deepest self."

"Art is a truth, after all," said Bronwyn, who had recently had her hair permed and could just catch the edges of it on the edges of her sightline. From that day on they were firm friends, and soon the friendship was a romantic friendship, which meant they touched each other a lot.

Esther lit her room with a red lightbulb. Bronwyn thought it rather crass, but would never have said so. Esther showed Bronwyn her sketchbook. Bronwyn didn't like the drawings. "They're so . . . mystical," she said. "Why don't you go to art school?"

"I didn't like it there," said Esther. "There were too many . . . there was too much . . . it was too constrained, there was no freedom of expression. I believe that Art is a bird which must be let out of a cage. I believe it is cruel to pick flowers. They ought to live and breathe, wild and free."

"Oh yes!" Bronwyn exclaimed, "yes, I believe that too." Bronwyn had a piece of meat stuck in one of her back teeth, and she poked and contorted with her tongue to free it. They sat there in the red glow, the sketchbook open on the floor between them. Esther thought how silly Bronwyn looked. "I like having my room a different colour," she said. "It gives me a new perception of things. I like seeing things in a new light."

"Oh I do too!" said Bronwyn.

Esther and Bronwyn sent each other letters most days; Bronwyn told Esther that this was what you did. The letters talked of trees and grass and the beauty of a bird singing close by. Esther illustrated her letters; Bronwyn stuck the letters on her bedroom wall with blu-tak. She said to people who called round, "These are from Esther, she's my artist friend, she's very interesting." The sink in Bronwyn's room made an ugly noise when the water ran out. She asked the landlord if there was anything he could do about it. He said he doubted it.

One night Esther came round with a new painting. They looked at it for a while, then had some tea and went out for a walk. Bronwyn slipped her arm through Esther's and recited poetry to her. The trees swayed above them, they walked by the river. Esther talked of how the trees reminded her of the Champs Elysées, Bronwyn agreed, although she had never been. Esther said she would have to go; they would go next summer. "Wonderful!" said Bronwyn. "The Champs Elysées smells of perfume on August evenings," said Esther with her eyes closed.

Then Esther painted Bronwyn nude, it took all afternoon, a cold afternoon of not being able to move, sitting on a chaise longue with only one bar of the electric fire on; Esther had very little money left on her grant. Bronwyn looked at the picture as she buttoned her blouse. Then she buttoned her skirt.

"Don't you like it?" said Esther, one eyebrow raised, white paint all down one arm.

"Don't you think you've made the breasts a little too big?" asked Bronwyn.

"They're supposed to be big," said Esther. "They are big."

"Well, it all depends on your perception," said Bronwyn. She shivered at Esther's perception of her breasts, and went to the bathroom to put on the rest of her clothes.

SEVEN POEMS

by Alison Smith

IN TOUCH

I phone and joke and in between the lines
lie miles of dark land, cities piercing thick
dark, flashing like dark-sky-spark stars. You, quick,
fire back; electric; I laugh, you laugh — fine
if we connect, if we can navigate
the distance with these tin-thin wisecracks, fight
the nervousness with this self-conscious wit,
each conscious that there's something to but what;
like when eyes chance on eyes, hand brushes hand
and we both (I think) spark and tingle (that's
the current-running question), understand
something that we can't say. Circling like cats
around a possibility that might,
nervened, we touch together almost quite.

BLOODY SILLY IF YOU ASK ME NOW

I placed the knife against my chest.
I really thought it for the best.
Thank God I didn't push it through.
It would have made an *awful* mess.

CARPE DIEM ON MONDAY IN THE PERIODICALS ROOM

Skirting round the edges of you,
feigning a politeness as you
talk about — I can't remember —
other things and other people,
what you did on Sunday evening,
what you're reading opposite me,
knowing that there's nothing that I
want more than to
touch your skin,
to feel you breathing sudden in,
to trace my finger down the thin
straight spine of you,
oh, fine, oh, you —

no, not the sort of thing that you
can safely do in libraries
to people that you hardly know.

I wonder if you think it too.

(come live with me and be my love
and touch my thigh under the table)

How the immediacy of it
eclipses all these books of walls;
how the thought of the touch can split
the mind into such breathing pieces,
the body into jumps and guesses,
make momentary into all;
this game we play of touch and go.

WHAT HAPPENS

Together we watch Dynasty.
It's where we find an easy line
of contact, where at least we find
each other, easy, company.

You grin and raise an eyebrow, sigh
at bits in beds or bare in showers.
I watch from well behind the covers
(intelligent) of some book or other

you won't have read and wouldn't want to,
and even if you did you couldn't;
"I sat and read for hours on end
before I had the five of you

and now I couldn't concentrate."
I turn another page, you knit
the jumper for the latest baby,
together, then, we watch the plot.

Photographs of you, the forties,
beautiful and energetic,
this one with your head back, laughing,
long neck, won a competition
in your local newspaper
before your father died, and there
could be no college without money.

There's this one I like too, of you
at sixteen, maybe seventeen
before you even met our dad,
in busconductress uniform
swinging with one arm round the pole
at the door of a forties bus
heading towards the five of us,

me the 'surprise' at the far end
looking at photographs of you
before you'd seen yourself in them,

before you knew of five of us
whose bones were knit inside your own.

Between the black and white and now,
no time; a family that came
from nowhere, now nowhere to go.
You sit alone by the window
and wonder what is happening
and wonder what has happened,

what is this sudden desert, come
upon you even in your home,
a lostness in the furniture,
a lostness in the bone.

You put a teabag in a cup,
pour water in and poke it brown
with a teaspoon, and fill the cup with milk,
and you sit down.

I phone five hundred miles away,
your youngest, and all we can say
is Were you watching Dynasty?
You tell me all that happened.

BUDDY CAN YOU SPARE A

time?
It's twenty five past
bloody
three
kids playing
on the tip
and nothing coming
through the
post or in the
paper or the
pub more likely
well
why don't you
bloody
look instead of
watching programmes
for the kids
out playing
      circus owners
      nurses
      doctors
      teachers
      tailors
      soldiers
      sailors
      rich men
      poor men
      cops and
rubbish
for the
bloody
tea
I told you
twenty five past
bloody
three

SECRET ANNEXE

Prinsengracht
in Amsterdam
and in among the houses
there is one
where tourists clump
where soldiers thumped
and clumped
and gutted
and the shock
appears in eyes
of those who feel the fear
still hidden here
and a little girl
look
dressed in red
skips singing
throwing shadows
right across the page
and someone shaves her hair
and strips her bare
and sews a star into her skin
but she commands
the audience's
full attention
with her song
and suddenly a fiction's tangible,
words speak the truth
throw shadows
on the flickering film
of frightened people
with their shaven
flickering eyes
behind barbed wire
the celluloid
a naked yellow image
of our own humanity
and holidaying we

Wendy Barr

MYSTERY AT IVY MANOR

"The Rookery",
Hay Lane,
Gimmertown,
Yorks.

12th October 1831

Dearest Emilia,

Well! It is a strange turnabout of events to be sure! Myself, I can hardly believe it, though the living proof is before me daily in the form of my dear husband.

It is so long since I last wrote to you, and I trust you are well, and that Henry's gout vexes him not too severely. My papa is a great believer in the application of pig's lard and vinegar to any paining or offending bodily organ or member. My papa is, as you know, somewhat of an expert on medical matters, suffering from the dropsy and scrofula in his later years. Pray do tell Henry of this remedy, to be applied twice daily. (I once had the indignity of having pig's lard smeared upon my ear when I was indisposed with earache, and it entangled my ringlets most dreadfully!) You may see by this letter what high animal spirits I am in! I only wish I could say the same about my dear papa, who is unwell at present, with what the apothecary suspects is bubonic plague.

I know you will be in much agitation, however, to know how it all came about, and if you have a moment or two to spare from your dear maternal duties; and if the infants can be cajoled into sleep or stupefaction by whatever means (a drop of laudanum upon their dummies is a most efficacious remedy, which my papa swears by) you must settle yourself down in some quiet nook of the house, by a good fire, with tea and the toasting iron and crumpets to hand, and I will tell you all.

As you know, I had been in residence at Ivy Manor, employed in the capacity of governess to a rich family in ——shire, on the outskirts of a northern industrial town. My charge was a little boy,

45

Edward, who was well behaved, and I considered myself fortunate in my post. I had been in residence little more than two weeks, when I began to suspect that all was not well at Ivy Manor. My employer, Mr Blackstone, I had yet to meet, being out of the country in Madeira, on business. The only other occupant of the large and gloomy mansion was the housekeeper, Mrs Draper. She was a kindly old woman, though somewhat garrulous, and being of a quiet and introspective nature (except with you, my dearest friend) I confess I found her constant chatter sometimes irksome. However, I could not complain, since I was left much alone to wander in the silent house and large grounds that surrounded it, an occupation that suited well my solitary habits. It was on such a walk that I first caught sight of the mysterious lady, with whom my epistle is concerned.

It was a clear autumn day, as I took my daily walk through the grounds. On looking up to the sky to admire the flitting clouds, and blue prospect, my eyes fell upon a figure standing by the old tower, looking down at me. It was unquestionably that of a woman, but who? As far as I knew Mrs Draper and I were the only ladies in the house, and the figure was slim, whereas Mrs Draper is portly. The servants were not allowed above stairs, besides which, rumours of the strange lady said to haunt the rooms of Ivy Manor kept them from venturing abroad, alone. Was I looking at the strange lady? But she surely was flesh and blood. The sun was behind the figure, so I could not see her face. I called to her, and she turned and disappeared behind the battlements of the tower.

That evening Mrs Draper and I sat by the fire in the parlour having tea. It was a wild and stormy night, and hailstones clattered on the panes of the large windows.

"Mrs Draper," I began, "is there any other lady besides ourselves in the house?"

"Why no, dear, whyever should you ask?"

"This afternoon," I began, "I fancied I saw a figure of a woman behind the battlements of the north tower."

"Why, Sarah, you must be mistaken, there is only ourselves and the master and as you know he is away on business at present . . . which reminds me," said she, "I have received word that the master will be coming home tomorrow, so there is much work to be done."

I must have looked perplexed, for she added, "Do not concern yourself, my dear, it is perhaps better not to listen to servants' talk; it was perchance a servant you saw upon the tower, for there is a strange woman among them who is often unwell, due to her own fault . . . I mean . . ." Mrs Draper appeared discomfited. "She often has recourse to the cooking brandy — there now! It is in part the fault of Mr Blackstone's good nature. He keeps her on out of kindness, I believe." Mrs Draper then contented herself planning the arrangements for the master's return, and I, half-listening, stared at the fire, leaving off my embroidery while I mused over the strange lady, the waggish cook, and the character of Mr Blackstone.

"So!" you will say, dearest Emilia, "the mystery is explained — it is the intemperate cook who haunts towers and peers down at my dear little friend." But wait my dear one, stay your hand from the servant's bell, to ring for the children, for tea, for the pony and trap to go a-visiting, there is more to come.

"Oh Sarah!" said Mrs Draper, bustling into my room, "you must put on your best dress and come down to the parlour, the master wishes to be entertained."

It was the evening of the following day, and again I had encountered the mysterious lady. That evening I had heard the swish of a silk gown glide past my half-open door, and rushing out, caught sight of the lady, disappearing up the stairs that led to the top storey. I called to her, but the sound of my voice appeared only to hasten her retreat.

"Why, Sarah," remonstrated Mrs Draper, giving my arm a sound pinch, "you are dreaming . . . come, you must make haste . . . you must allow me to dress you, in the best dress you have."

Before long, I was ushered into the master's presence. He sat in an arm-chair, staring thoughtfully at the fire, a glass of brandy warming in his hand. A large fire burned in the grate, illuminating his features in pink radiance. (You observe, I wax lyrical . . . Alas! my master, my *dear* master inspires such in me!) He did not look up as I entered, giving me leave to study him.

"Miss Grey is here," announced Mrs Draper.

"Tell me, Miss Grey," said the master, staring at the fire as if the very flames had hypnotized him, "do you 'oft have fancy ludicrous and wild . . . trees, strange visages expressed in the red cinders . . .', do you care for fire staring?"

A show of formality, of finished politeness, would have undone me, but his behaviour, albeit eccentric to some (Mrs Draper looked at a loss) pleased me. I liked it well.

"Yes, and Cowper is also my favourite poet," I said, not without a little vanity. He raised his eyes. His features were coarse, but not ugly. Rather they were manly and formidable, the way a rock is

47

formidable. His eyes blazed into my own, but I met his gaze with my own steady look, outwardly calm as always.

"You are a strange one, Miss Grey. Where is the flutter, the clutching of a bead purse, the shake of an impatient fan? Does my behaviour not discompose you? See how it sits, its little hands folded on its lap, (where I would long to lay my weary head, were we not fettered by meaningless niceties, the manners of polite society!), those large honest eyes, fixed upon my own! Why *you* have unsettled me! Are you a changeling, an elf, come to torment me with your honest, searching eyes? I have no secrets, I tell you, none!"

Mr Blackstone appeared in much agitation, whether from too much port at dinner, or the brandy in his hand, I could not tell. I turned my gaze from him to the large mirror above the mantelpiece, and observed the chandelier blazing brightly within it.

Mr Blackstone collected himself. "Sit down here, Miss Grey, where I can see you better," he indicated a chair dangerously near his own. "You will forgive me if I do not rise — I have been so long out of the society of women that my manners have grown brutish. Mrs Draper, you may leave us. I wish to interview Miss Grey alone. Kindly retire to the kitchen."

The good matron looked a trifle put out, but obeyed, and I heard her mutter, "Well I never, in all my born days . . ." as she closed the doors. We were alone.

"Tell me, Miss Grey, how do you find me? You study me so that, were I a lesser man, I would shrink from your gaze. Do you think me handsome?"

"No, sir," I replied.

"No indeed! Ha ha," he laughed. "Why, she shows spirit behind that quiet grey exterior," he said, half to himself.

"I am bored, Miss Grey, and I wish to be entertained." Here he paused. "Tell me Miss Grey, can you dance the Can-Can?"

I replied that I could not.

"Forgive me," he said, laughing. "I am shortly returned from Paris; I hope you realise that I am a drunken reprobate, Miss Grey, and that those dresses and pretty ladies quite mesmerized me."

You may wonder, gentle Emilia, what my thoughts were that night, on retiring to my own chamber, regarding Mr Blackstone. I will leave you to your conjectures; suffice to say that I found him interesting.

The following day, my charge, Edward, was unusually restless at his lessons.

"Why Edward," I asked, "whatever is the matter with you, you who are usually such a good student?" He stood at the nursery window, his nose pressed to the glass.

"I want to see the lady again," came his somewhat nasal reply.

"Which lady?" I asked. "Do you mean Mrs Draper?"

"No, not Mrs Draper, the other lady."

I came over to the window where Edward stood. From the nursery window, we had a view of another part of the house, and there, in a room at the top storey, stood the lady, silhouetted in the window. She wore a black dress, not unlike my own, and a lace cap upon her head. She looked strangely familiar, but I reasoned that this was because I had, of late, often caught sight of her.

Now, my dear Emilia, you must draw across the heavy curtains of your room — first, see how the autumn light falls so prettily upon the carpet, but linger not at the window to observe the trees in the park, the serving girl scrubbing the steps of number 17, the nurse walking past with her perambulator, wherein sits the hope and dreams of Mr and Mrs Pettigrew, 10 Clovelly Mansions, undistinguishable at this moment from other dribbling infants; let not these things detain you, but bolt and secure the door, and settle down again in that friendly old arm-chair, with your feet upon the fender, for I now reach the conclusion, the denouement of my strange tale.

That evening, after tea, I resolved to go to that room in the third storey, to see if I could unravel the mystery. I was unafraid, for after all was she not a creature of my own sex? What harm could she do me? While Mrs Draper dozed and snored by the parlour fire, (Papa's remedy for recalcitrant infants again proving useful), the glass of hot negus I had prepared for her lying half-tasted on the table by her arm, I gently relieved her of the bunch of household keys strung on a belt around her waist. I made my way to the room wherein I had seen the lady that afternoon from the nursery. Eventually I managed to find the right key and let myself softly into the chamber. It smelled old and dusty from little use, and the only furniture was a large ornate full-length mirror, and a huge mahogany wardrobe. I opened the door of the wardrobe. The room was uncannily quiet, and the wardrobe door opened with a slow creaking sound that shattered the stillness. Inside, there was a riot of colour, of blues and turquoise, of red and green. The sight was quite dazzling to my eyes, and it took me some seconds to determine that the colours were in fact dresses, ball gowns, riding outfits; in short enough clothes to suit an empress. On the top shelf were wigs and hair-pieces, bottles of scent and pomade, and arsenic cream for skin-lightening. I was so absorbed in contemplating the scene before me that I did not hear the sound of footsteps advancing along the hallway — I heard a rattle at the door and with alacrity I ran to the large window and concealed myself behind its commodious drapes, frightened, yet curious to know who the lady was.

Imagine my surprise, dear reader, when Mr Blackstone entered the room. His hair was blown about his face, and his eyes had a wild, unseeing look.

He spoke aloud to the empty air, "I must try one more, I must try the pretty little lilac one."

He made his way to the wardrobe and pulled out a lilac dress, and walked to the mirror, holding the dress up in front of him. He let out a sigh of satisfaction, as he turned this way and that, to see what it would look like.

Here I blush, gentle Emilia, to tell you that Mr Blackstone began swiftly to disrobe. With due propriety, I averted my eyes until he had attired himself in the lilac gown. So Mr Blackstone was the mysterious lady! I could scarcely believe my eyes. I realised then the significance of his interest in the pretty ladies and their dresses in Paris! I revealed myself, stepping out from the curtain.

"Mr Blackstone, you are discovered!" I cried.

His face turned, aghast.

"Miss Grey . . . how . . . did you find this room . . . oh! . . . I am undone!"

"Yes, you are undone, sir," I cried, and then went over to fasten his buttons at the back, which in his eagerness he had neglected.

Dearest Emilia, I married him. The ceremony was performed in a little parish church in ——shire. I keep Mr Blackstone's secret to myself, (and urge you to do the same), and in private we have many amusing moments choosing dresses to wear and planning our colour schemes. He is a good and kind husband, and I consider myself most fortunate. Alas, I wish with all my heart the same could be said of Papa! Since the writing of this letter, he has contracted St Vitus Dance, and does whirl and turn about the floor most pitifully. However, the apothecary, Mr Blunder, is of the opinion that Papa does not have bubonic plague, and that sea-bathing and cold gruel would soon set his latest indisposition to rights — so that is a blessing. We must be grateful for small mercies.

I am *very* happy, dear Emilia, my only sorrow is that you could not be my bridesmaid, but as you will no doubt understand, the ceremony had to be conducted in great secrecy, since we both wore bride's attire. (My spouse looked quite fetching in his white veil!)

Hark! I think I hear my dear one call me. We are choosing our winter wardrobe, and both think muslin a sound choice, being light and fashionable at present. Well my dear, I must leave you and attend to my caro sposo. All my love to Henry, little Arabella and Frederick.

> I remain,
> Your faithful and loving friend,
> Mrs Sarah Blackstone (née Grey).

Iris Doyle

AN ALTERNATIVE ROMANCE

Well, who would have thought it would come to this. Cleary and I sitting across from each other, he in a flowered print dress, a whiskey in his hand and me in a chair, sipping away on my gin.

I call him Cleary *now*. He was tired of being George. He said it was dull. Well, he certainly isn't dull now. No, you should see him sitting here, bright rosy colours flounced about his legs. No wait . . . don't cut off in disgust. Give Cleary a chance. That's all George told me he wanted when he made his grand dénouement. "Give me a *chance*," he said, a vague plea in the eye. Well, as I picked myself up off the floor and reeled about the kitchen in a stupor a *chance* I didn't think George, or rather, Cleary, had. I know all this changing of names is confusing but stick with it, just remember that George and Cleary are the same person and if you think *that's* difficult you'll be able to share in my plight even more. It's not been easy. I have felt very martyred at times, but I rush on here, at the risk of confusing you even more. Just visualize Cleary and I sitting here with our drinks. We're sitting here sipping on the booze, giving it all its little chance.

Of course my mother will never forgive him, said she'd known all along that there was something odd about George and she *begs* me never to bring him near her neighbourhood. I understand, after all, it was her nighties he had pinched but I really don't think she's trying to take in a wider view of the issue. She thanks God my father's dead now. I thank God that something brought her out of her martyred widowhood but I wish it hadn't been George.

I suppose George is right, George is a boring name but where does it leave me? If George is boring, Irene tags along after it a near contender. But let's not start splitting hairs over the simple aspects of this matter — what of the rest? My mother said that her sister Betty vomited when she heard. They had been sitting eating cheesecake and Betty vomited. Very visual. Betty said I could go and stay with her anytime. Not with George in tow of course. She said she wasn't risking Aids from dirt like George. I did explain to mother that wearing frocks wouldn't actually transmit the disease and that she mustn't get transvestism confused with homosexuality. No doubt *some* homosexuals do wear frocks, *I* don't know the bloody statistics but it was all sheets flapping in the wind because my mother told me not to talk filthy, informing me she would tell Betty nothing of the kind and what sort of gratitude was this that I was showing Betty anyway. God. But all this isn't the point, the point is George, or rather, Cleary.

You'll want to know how George actually conveyed the fact that he was into frocks and frillies. It was simple. He came home one day, disappeared for a while — I was in the kitchen doing the lasagne — and reappeared at the table wearing one of mother's nighties. We had thought it had been taken from her washing line by a pervert but there it was on George. Pale blue with pleated tucks at the shoulder and a ribbon round the neckline. We'd bought it for her birthday. Mind you, in some quirky way, the shock of seeing the nightie again did somehow dampen the shock of seeing George wearing it. The mind's a fabulous thing, it jumps hither and thither to cope with the unusual. My mind lapsed into automatic pilot so I didn't get hit with the full flood of events head on. It was when my sights had raised from the nightie to George's face that I really had to take in that things had changed. Cosmetics. George had on cosmetics. I know that's nothing to sway about about, but it annoyed me a bit that *he* was wearing what he objected to *me* wearing. I know, I know, least of my problems, but as I say, the mind is a wonderful thing, it hopscotches to protect, it gave me an irk to blot out my bigger worry.

Anyway, I sat down, served out the lasagne and said: "Well." Is *that* not the master of understatement? You see, some fool of a little man was tap-dancing about my brain by this time. I was dumb, I admit it, I was dumb as a duck as I ate my lasagne, sneaking looks at George. I'll say this for George, he was cool. Not a quiver. Of course he was in his *Cleary* persona then so that probably made the difference. I have to hand it to Cleary. Cleary is smooth as glass. No beating of the breast or soul searching there. Not a bit of it. He even had a bit of a smirk playing about his mouth. But, back to the beginning. At the end of this lasagne meal (you know, I can't *touch* lasagne now), George tells me, or rather Cleary tells me, that this is to be a permanent *thing*. "Mother's nighties?" I asked, dreading the answer, but that, at least, I was to be spared. The nighties weren't to be permanent, it was just that these were the only clothes he could get into, in future he would get proper clothes. (Mother will never forgive the fact that he started out in her nighties . . . she says she feels she's been raped.) Yes, proper clothes were to be bought for Cleary.

Hyteria forced me to ask if he knew how much all this would cost, as though *that* was the only price we would have to pay. George said he would get a bank loan. My mind reeled.

George said he could tolerate work days in the confines of his male garb, that he would endure the restrictions then as he didn't think Mr Brown (his boss) would be able to take him in frocks and anyway it would be hard to crawl about under cars or peer into their engines in a dress. I found myself agreeing with him (as if there were a choice to be considered), as he explained all this. He would suffer at work, but he could no longer be imprisoned in his own home. That's the word he used. Imprisoned. I pointed out that it was my home too, but Cleary was too busy to listen. Cleary was busy telling me how much he hated George.

George was *dull*, George *conformed*, George was *trapped*. George was the one thing that George didn't want to be anymore. I said, with a touch of bitterness, that I wished I wasn't Irene anymore, but it sailed right past him. He had reached a natural high. He was killing off George. And when I heard the way Cleary described him I don't say I blame him, he sounded like a pain. I even sat wondering how *I* had stood George for so long as he told me all about Cleary. He wanted to be Cleary. Cleary had *charm*, Cleary was *smooth*, Cleary was a *rebel*, Cleary was *exciting*, Cleary *was*. I would never have guessed that George knew so many adjectives, but there I had it. I had it neatly laid out on the line. I was living with two men. George the dullard and Cleary who was at one with himself. George and Cleary. (And don't talk to me of greed.)

And you'll be wondering just where George got the name Cleary from? He told me it came to him in a dream. He said that he had been in this dream, a bright, exciting person, running down a road with yards of chiffon trailing out behind him and he heard a beautiful voice calling after him. The voice was calling Cleary. He said he ran down this dream with the chiffon and the hypnotic voice calling and when he woke he had such a sense of grief that there was no chiffon and no Cleary that he decided *he would become Cleary*. Cleary had stuck with him. Now Cleary is stuck with me. The chiffon has stuck too. He now has many chiffon frocks, like the Queen Ma, only different.

And he's joined a club. They all meet on Wednesdays and swop information about tights, who sells the largest sizes, cosmetics, and how awful it is that none of their families understand them. It just goes to show that there's a self-help group for everything now. I even saw a poster in the library for an agoraphobics self-help group. They were to meet on a Thursday, but how the hell were they to get there? But then, that's their problem, Cleary's mine.

Yes, they say that no one understands them. The trouble is we understand them only too well. They want to dress up in frocks and high shoes and be who they aren't. Who doesn't want to be someone else? I told George that one night. I said: "George . . . there's not a person alive who wants to be who they are and if they do say they want to be who they are they're lying . . ." George said that this proved I didn't understand. I don't know just how he worked that out from what I said, but he did. Or, rather, Cleary did, because by this time George was Cleary for approximately fifteen hours out of every day and George for only the eight hours he was at work plus the hour that he spent travelling to and from work. So I didn't see much of George at all by this time, I just caught a glimpse of him as he slunk in or out of the house. It wasn't easy. Nothing was easy anymore.

In the beginning my mother would call round every day asking what I was planning to do about George, but she stopped calling the day she arrived and it was a Bank Holiday and George was at home being Cleary in a little spotted number. What a shock it had been to her. She'd grasped her neck with one hand, covered her mouth with the other one, and started breathing funny. She doesn't call round anymore. She phones instead and asks me what I'm going to do about George.

At one point she suggested a psychiatrist, but I pointed out that it was only worth while going to a shrink if George wanted to dump Cleary and become George again full time, but since this wasn't the case it hardly seemed sensible to spend time asking our doctor to refer us to a specialist just so that George could tell him that he was very happy being a transvestite thank you very much. Shrinks don't want to see you because you're happy. My mother asked why I was taking George's side on this matter. I pointed out that it wasn't a case of *sides*, it was just a matter of *fact*, but she wasn't convinced and said that if I wasn't willing to see about a shrink for George maybe I should see about getting a lawyer. Then when she imagined George and I up in court getting the marriage put to sleep while some grubby little journalist scraped down in his little notebook what colour of frock George was wearing, she decided that going to a lawyer wasn't, after all, the best way to handle things. She was stumped. Then Betty had put the idea into her head that George would probably be going for a sex change operation next and that sent her into a spin, but I conveyed her fear to Cleary, and Cleary assured me that he had no desire to go under the knife to bring about a transformation since it wasn't the female form he desired — just the feel of all those feminine garments. I told her this, she said she felt sick. Cleary would toss her attitudes at me as further proof that no one understood.

No one understood, except, of course, the people in the self-help group. If you ask me they helped themselves a bit too much. Not only did they indulge each other and hand out sympathy all round, but they organised little trips for themselves. They've been to the theatre, been on a historical tour of some little known stately home and even (it doesn't bear thinking about) held little birthday parties for various members of the group in a local pub where they all took their gifts of perfume and earrings. Cleary loves earrings. He had his ears pierced a month ago and just lives for the day the little studs can come out and he can start wearing danglers. I told my mother that at least George's new situation would simplify buying Christmas gifts; after all, last year she had been so stuck for ideas of what to buy George she had ended up getting him a ten-thousand-piece jigsaw puzzle. Now we could get him earrings or perfume or little trinkets for the charm bracelet he now wears, but she missed the point.

But I was telling you about Cleary's self-help group. There are five of them: Grace, Ruth, Margey, Alison and Cleary. Cleary is the only one that doesn't have a female name and the others in the group were a mite confused about this in the beginning, but since Cleary relayed the tale of the wonderful dream they understand. They understand everything. Apparently Ruth kept crying all the time because she is really huge and she worried about never being able to pretend to be petite and pretty, but they even understood that, and Margey sent away for a catalogue from a firm that deals in outsize ladies' clothing and this has helped Ruth no end. See the kind of people they are?

And you wouldn't believe the trouble they have getting things to fit. I told my mother this; she said maybe *I* should see the shrink instead of George, which was ridiculous because I was only pointing out to her that Cleary was crippling himself because he couldn't find a pair of stilettos that would fit. OK I'm none too pleased about the situation, but there's no point in me becoming a bitch as I watch Cleary limp out to his group on a Wednesday night, is there?

Yes, he does actually go out in his Cleary garb. And yes, the neighbours do see him. And yes, they are shocked. My mother asks how I can hold my head up. It isn't easy. Pat and Brian, who live next door, used to call round for a drink, but Pat said that Brian is convinced that George is a poof, and anyway what would his darts team think if they heard about him having a drink with George? I assured her that Cleary was not, in any way, gay; she believed me, but said that Brian didn't, so we don't see them anymore. We see the members of the group though, they call round, so what we've lost in one way we've gained in another. Ours is the only house they can come to. Apparently none of the other wives will let them call. My mother said that I would be the fool that let them call. I pointed out to Cleary that this provided further evidence of just how understanding I was, but he said that even if I hadn't wanted them round *he* would have and since it was *his* house anyway there wasn't much I could do about it. You see, a man's a man even when he's in a frock. There he was being very mucho macho and going on about *his* possessions. One would have thought . . . but no . . . that's getting away from the point. The point is that the little group now call round and there I am, the fool, serving coffee and drinks and comparing notes about colours and sizes in the hope of winning through in some way. I serve and parley and giggle alongside them and wonder how I came to possess four new friends, or five, if you count Cleary as being new. My mother wonders how I can do it.

But wait, *you'll* wonder by now how I can do it. You'll wonder why I don't leave Cleary, or rather, leave George and let him get on with his Cleary business solo. You'll wonder why I don't tell him to sling his heels and get together with his little group permanent, because he's not getting together with me anymore. You'll wonder why I don't run round to Betty's, weep on her shoulder and listen to my mother telling me that she was right after all. You'll wonder many things. I wondered them too. Then I sat with my George and Cleary lists ticking off the good points about George and the bad points about George in an attempt to weigh up if it was worth putting in more mileage with him. Then I tallied up the list that dealt with the pluses and the minuses of the Cleary persona. I've got to tell you . . . Cleary won hands down. George was *dull*, George did *conform*, George was *trapped*, and on Cleary's list we had words like *smooth* and *charm* and *exciting*. George was a non-starter. Cleary *was*.

So here we sit across from each other, Cleary in his flowered print dress, and me in my chair sipping my gin.

And anyway . . . we couldn't let my mother think she was right.

POEMS

by Joy Pitman

SALES PATTER

sorry
I don't deal
in parts
this item comes complete
no dis-embodied spirits
and you can't unplug my heart
the body's integral
you'll have to take the package
whole

and by the way
you'll need to treat with care
they haven't worked out yet
a way to make
replacements

FANTASY

Each time I fantasise what I might say
I'm sure of your reply
But in reality you won't have learnt
Your lines as well as I.

POEM FOR TRAMPOLINE

that art of falling on your bottom
and bouncing back
consists mainly in not trying

— just a knack

life has its ups and downs

FIVE CYNICAL SONGS

I

Oh you don't want me
I'd be faithful and true,
No you don't want me
I'd demand things of you.

Oh I don't want you
For you can't see
And you wouldn't be true
To yourself or to me.

Oh no I don't want you.
But I want you
To want me
But I want you
But I want
But.

II

I'm disenchanted
midnight's gone
no more dancing
with masked partners
so don't come round
with empty slippers
this Cinderella's going to keep
her feet upon the ground

even if she still enjoys
a fairy-tale at bedtime.

III

Don't worry dear, you've made it clear
You're weary of love's game.
Just keep your mask impassive
I won't insist you play
And when you've cut the last link through
I'll put my heart away.

Now — let's talk of other things.

IV

last season's love
has faded fast
and this year's styles
aren't made to last
sincerity goes out of fashion
and honesty grows thin
so I'll wear my cynicism longer
and tuck my trust well in.

V

let's be
carefully
care free

Helen Lamb

POINTED TOES

On the day he finally became dispensable, his wife went out and bought three new pairs of shoes. They pleased her so much that, for almost a week, she couldn't keep her eyes off her feet. She walked lightly — pointing her toes in different directions, and standing in experimental poses. The low, black pumps were cleverly cut at the front to make her feet look a couple of sizes smaller — four-and-a-half or five at the most. They were so dainty she felt like a geisha girl. She stood with her toes pointed outwards and considered taking up ballet again. She had bought the emerald green sandals in a sale. Perhaps they were too exotic. She decided to paint her toenails fuschia pink. The effect was outrageous. But the stilettos were the best — three-and-a-half inches high, in classic navy. She liked to listen to them click as she walked down the street. It was a very satisfying noise.

The husband admired the shoes, and suggested some new clothes. A dress, perhaps. She should wear more. He made appreciative noises about her shape. This unexpected interest made her edgy. He didn't usually notice what she wore. Then, he infuriated her by apologising for the hard times — as though it was his fault he had lost his job. She wished he wouldn't be so nice. She had just blown a week's pay on the shoes. Why didn't he shout at her. It was unfair of him to take all the blame. She wouldn't let him. He was being greedy — selfish masquerading as selfless. She would prefer to dispose of the guilt altogether, like her worn-out shoes. The dustbin was the place for lost causes. And anyway, why should he get the credit for her misery? It was her own.

She said, "Let's call it quits." And he knew that she was quitting on more than just hard times.

The wife was pleasant but remote. She had grown to be so comfortably self-contained. Her life revolved around her job, her home, her plants, her books, her friends. She took a dance class twice a week. There was no room for change — no room for him. When he spoke to her, she smiled, but her eyes glanced past him to something beyond. She said no more than was necessary and seemed startled when he entered a room, as though she had forgotten he was in the house.

Three days a week the wife went to work. They needed the money now. Without her, the house became unrecognisable. It seemed to him that the furniture, the lamps, the plants, even the crockery had been carefully arranged according to some mysterious plan. Only she knew why. He couldn't relax and spent his days waiting for her to come back. After a while, he began to change a few things around. Nothing much to start with. The first time, he moved the settee to face the fire and placed a low table next to it. Then he put a lamp and some of his books on the table. His wife was late. He put his feet up on the settee and waited for her to return. When she did get home, she said a quick hello and disappeared into the kitchen, refusing his offers of help. She made no comment on the changes.

He couldn't bear the isolation. In an attempt to get her attention, he cranked up old, mechanical arguments and tossed them into the kitchen like grenades. He criticised the food. Was she not aware that saturated fats clogged up the arteries? She offered to make him a salad. Not only that, saturated fats were politically immoral. Meat production was a waste of resources. A major cause of food shortages in the third world. He could not understand her aversion to brown rice.

She agreed with him. Her dislike of brown rice was irrational. Did he want mayonnaise on his salad?

He examined the label and said he would sooner eat horse shit.

She laughed and said, "Well, at least that's natural."

He took this as a criticism. She was always telling him not to be so neurotic about what he ate. He accused her of intolerance. She was stupid — self-satisfied. She wondered why he didn't just accuse her of trying to poison him and be done with it. But, for once, she didn't say it. He said that she had no idea what was going on out there in the real world — again.

She didn't respond. Where had she gone? She didn't even slam the door as she went out. This wife, who used to hurl back the most venomous abuse — double tit for tat — had suddenly declared a unilateral truce. Disarmed, he was bewildered.

The wife became vague and forgetful. Sometimes, he caught her staring into space. When he asked what she was thinking she said "nothing much", and looked at him strangely, as though she couldn't figure out what he was doing there. There were such a lot of things she couldn't remember. She couldn't remember what it felt like to be with another man — the adrenalin, the tension, the unfamiliar rhythm and scent. She couldn't remember what it felt like to have a whole bed to herself — the sensation of cool cotton sheets on a hot night, with no one to stick to and no one to remind her to put out the light. And, even more important, she couldn't remember when she had stopped wanting to with him all the time. She used to resent his going to work. She would drag him back to bed, make him late and spend her days waiting for him to come home again. And now he was there all day, she only felt sorry for him.

It made his wife uncomfortable to see him suddenly slumped. She had relied on this man. But, he was, after all, no stronger than her. Maybe weaker. One thought nagged at her — that she may have sapped his strength and taken if for herself — shades of Samson and Delilah. She felt a heavy pain behind her eyes, but couldn't cry.

Once, she told him that she found it difficult to believe that he actually worked when he was away from her. It seemed preposterous. All he ever mentioned was the office patter, the coffee breaks and disruptions. He couldn't believe she was saying this. What did a draughtsman do all day? Ten years on the job and she still had no idea what he did. He hadn't told her about the day-in, day-out boredom of it all. He hadn't mentioned the fact that, every Sunday night, for the past ten years, he had considered chucking it in. No — he definitely hadn't told her that. And now, he hated her for not knowing.

The winter came and went silently. They moved around each other with caution. Her face said, "Do not disturb". And he didn't try. He was tired. It was a chilling peace, accustomed as they were to the everyday hostilities.

And then, one night, he nudged her out of feigned sleep. "Look. Up there — a moving light in the sky. What is it?" He whispered urgently in the dark.

She sat up, rubbing her eyes. "I can't see anything. Maybe it was a plane. The airport's over in that direction."

"No. It's still there. Why can't you see it?" She heard the rasp of rising exasperation in his voice and tried to look harder.

"Look." He put an arm around her shoulder. "Try to follow the line my finger's pointing in. Now — take a leap straight out into the black. Don't let your gaze wander. Can you see it — out there coming in from the stars, red and green and violet lights?"

Ah yes. She could see it now.

"It can't be a star. It's too near." He whispered in her ear so as not to disturb the huge forces of space and time. As if the light might stop in its tracks, sensing the naked man and woman, huddled together, eavesdropping on the universe through a picture window.

They lay awake, one cool skin skimming the surface of the other and, as they watched, the light appeared to rotate and move towards them. They speculated on what it could be. Perhaps the pulsating lights were a signalling code.

She wished it would come to them quickly.

The violet light sent out messages of hope. She was sure of that. The green seemed to growing in power. It throbbed out healing rays. And, the red light augured something quite new that couldn't be named or imagined, though they would both try anyway.

They watched for hours — wide eyed, inviting galaxies to roll inside — until, at last their eyeballs couldn't take the strain. The light got no closer and they subsided to make love in the cold dawn light.

Their bodies seemed nebulous. "I could put my hand right through his chest," she thought. "He would feel no pain — only the vaguest sensation of bodies floating within bodies, overlapping spaces."

That night, they didn't roll apart to their separate dreams. They rested lightly together, uncovered to the waist. And, as his head grew heavy on her breast, her last thought was that he always spotted the magic first. Maybe she needed him just for that and nothing else.

It was Venus they had seen. The following day he called her at work, just to tell her. He was so enthusiastic it made her want to cry. She turned away from her colleagues and fixed her gaze on her feet. She was wearing the classic navy stilettos. The heels felt a bit rocky now and the toes were scuffed. She thought that nothing — good or bad — lasts forever, and wondered if they were worth repairing. When her husband finally said goodbye, she put down the phone and went back to work wishing it was five o'clock.

THREE POEMS

by Christine Cherry

SHE SWALLOWED FLOWERS

She swallowed flowers of bitterness
the seeds fell on a ledge
above a chasm
and rooted.
She cannot forget, she cannot remember.

Roots stretch down through the earth
of her body and each year
about this time
shoots spring against resistance
and the shadow of a bright bloom
explodes uncomfortably inside her head.

I'D FORGOTTEN HOW IT FEELS

I'd forgotten how it feels
to stand where the river tips over
the edge of land, naked
afraid to look where the water
falls sheer,
deep into the whirlpool's core.

I'd forgotten how it feels
to be opened like a spring sky
reason scattered by the wind,
yearning
filled with clouds fit to burst
and stretch themselves
across horizons red with sun.

A WEDNESDAY AFTERNOON

A wednesday afternoon in July
afloat amongst the pillows,
time expands around us
and would bear us down its rippled way.

I see the room reflected in your glasses
shades of red and blue; chaos of papers
the casual drape of a shirt.
Our two way mirror rocks upon its hinge.

Two dreamers getting along.

Wilma Murray

OLD WIVES' TALES

That, kiddo, was called a contraction. No doubt about it now.
So. This is it, then.

It's just you and me now. Till birth us do part.

Don't get scared. I reckon we have a few hours left to ourselves before we have to tell anyone. And I need the time. Okay? You see, while the world is turning ever so casually on its axis, I am about to be slipped into a supporting role for the rest of my life to leave you the centre stage. It may be the first day of your life, but it's the last day of my childhood. So give me a few hours to get used to the idea, eh?

That sounds selfish. I know. But don't fret. There'll be years and years ahead for me to worry about you.

I must say you haven't got much of a day for it. In fact, if I were at all superstitious and chose to believe the omens like grandma did, I can tell you they're not good. The sun's not even shining. There's a distinct smell of withering in the air this grey September morning. See, the roses are rotted with the rain and it looks like every pest in the book is busy chewing holes and spitting green. At least Fat-Cat's pleased. They've cut the barley and all the refugee mice have taken him completely by surprise this morning. He'll come in and present us with another little furry body in some advanced state of shock any time now. Stay where you are for a while. Have a last swim around in the warm dark. There's nothing out here for you today. No star in the east or three wise men for you, kiddo.

Funny how I thought I'd be ready for all this. Just a few more hours. Please? If you don't panic, I won't. But it's not how it was described in the manual.

Aww ... Jesus! Okay, okay. I'll see if I can get you one wise woman.

I told you. The world out here's not a place to rush into. There's AIDS, drugs and God knows what all lurking out here, colds and rotten teeth, acid rain and nuclear waste — all this in spite of the wonder of the modern world. (They can predict the return of Halley's comet with pinpoint accuracy, but they couldn't tell me when you would be born. Doesn't that seem odd to you?)

What else can I tell you about your chosen birth day, then? Well, Nelson Mandela is *still* in prison, there are killings in Northern Ireland, wars in three continents, famine in another, but, Coronation Street carries on. Women are spying on Greenham Common and picking brambles at the same time, pinning hopes on wholesome pies and laying down a future in jams and good strong wine. Just wait till you taste a bramble and apple pie!

It's a funny old world. And don't you go expecting me to explain it all away, either. I'll wipe your bum and put plasters on your knees, maybe teach you to play the piano and help you with your homework. After that, you're on your own, kiddo. Like the rest of us. Mummies can't kiss the world better any more and there ain't no fairy godmothers.

There are grandmas, though. They're the next best thing. They're good with the fairy tales, are grandmas. I have one of my own, so I know. Of course, you'll be seeing her soon. She's something else, that one. When I asked her — you know, woman to woman for the very first time — what it was like the day mother was born, she told me it was snowing! The omens seemed good for the times, she said. It was Winston Churchill's birthday and St Andrew's Day, so the flags were flying. Well, you had to keep your spirits up during the war, she said. She would tell my mother the flags were up for her and not worry her about things like war.

You could keep them ignorant then, you see. No TV. Anyway, she told me all of that, almost in one breath, but did not volunteer one word about the birth itself. She remembers the midwife's jokes and her bad feet, though. She patted my arm finally and said I'd forget about it as soon as it was over. That was a great help. And mother, she still can't bear to watch war documentaries or read about the Holocaust because she knows she spent the whole sorry six years skipping through other people's time. I teased her about grandma telling her the flags were for her and she gave me that look. The one that can tidy up a room.

Not that she was any great help either. When I asked her what it was like the day I was born, she said it was a scorcher and she just about died of thirst. My God! I should have thought that was the least of her problems. I persisted, but it's not easy asking your mother little questions like — how was your labour? She told me it took twenty-eight hours and the temperature outside rose to eighty at one point. Some kids at the local school sports collapsed with heatstroke, she remembers. I wasn't asking about the weather, dammit.

If you're a girl, I promise, I do, I promise that when the time comes

I'll tell you every last detail. Come to think of it, I'll tell you even if you're a boy. I'm all for equality.

In the end, she confided it wasn't too bad. Anyway, she said, it'll all be worth it. And that's it. That's the extent of the experience handed down through generations to me, now, with my big belly.

Hey! Is this hurting you as much as it's hurting me? Read the book, kiddo. This is supposed to be the good bit. So hang on to your hat, because here it comes again.

Holy. Hell!

I knew it. I just knew it. She was lying through her teeth. Twenty-eight hours she was in labour with me. Twenty-eight hours! And all she'll tell me is that it wasn't too bad. So what's bad? What are we registering on the Richter scale now, for example? I tell you, this is getting scary.

Where's that book?

Where's that bloody book?

Recite something, the book says. Quick.

> Humpty Dumpty sat on a wall
> Humpty Dumpty had a great fall
> All the King's horses
> And all the King's men
> Couldn't put Humpty together again.

That's going to go down well in the ambulance. Speaking of which, I'm going to phone them. Sorry, but I'm losing my grip, as they say, and it's your fault.

No, forgive me. That's not true. It's their fault. The secret society of mothers out there.

You okay in there? Just hold on a while yet, kiddo. Hey! I'll soon have to stop calling you that. You'll have a name. And all the other trappings of a statistic. They'll start a file on you and you'll get orange juice, an education and free dental treatment till you're sixteen. Then you'll get to collect Social Security like the rest of us. Just like your Dad. And if you're wondering where your other parent is at this critical juncture in your life, he's out looking for work, again. That's where he is. I sent him off this morning without telling him about the queer ache in my back that started all this. Well, he would only have fussed. He's a lovely man, though. You'll like him. I promise. But, if he doesn't find a job soon, you'll have that on your birth certificate, you know. Father — Unemployed.

This is not funny any more. I'm not sure I can take much more of it. WHY DIDN'T SOMEONE TELL ME?

> Humpty Dumpty sat on a wall
> Humpty Dumpty had a great fall . . .

Myself, I think he was conned. Just like me. Why else would an egg go and jump off a wall? Well, there's a lot of it about, I suppose. Conspiracy, that is. I did warn you it wasn't much of a world. Everybody's at it. Governments, drug companies, slimming magazines and that silly bitch who ran the ante-natal classes. To think I believed all that guff about clenched fists mimicking contractions. Remember? "Tighten. Clench. Ho-o-ld it. Re-lax." What a load of crap.

Just like mother and her "not too bad". Just like all of them, all the bloody mothers down all the bloody generations who have never told it as it is. THANK YOU FOR NOTHING ALL YOU MOTHERS OUT THERE.

Oh, but it will all be worth it, they say.

Oh? Will it really?

You'll forget about it as soon as it's over, they say.

No I won't. I'm going to spill the beans. I'm going to tell all. And I'm telling you, kiddo. This is hell.

This. This is the biggest con of them all. This is the lulu. This . . . Oh, God . . . I bet if someone asked the Virgin Mary what it was like the day Jesus was born, she'd say it was a fine clear night with plenty of stars.

I wonder if Jesus had a birth certificate? Father — God. Hah! Imagine trying to get that through the system today.

INPUT ERROR.

PLEASE RETYPE.

Don't worry, kiddo. You don't have a God in the family. You won't upset any of their computer programmes.

> Humpty Dumpty sat on a wall
> Humpty Dumpty had a great fall
> All the King's horses and all the King's men
> Couldn't put Humpty together again.

It has not escaped my notice how much I resemble an egg.

So.

It's time to go, kiddo.

Let's go jump off the wall.

THREE POEMS

by Christine Quarrell

KATHY THE CALEY QUEEN

I'm Kathy the Caley Queen
I'm doon tae five a day
I'v reared three wains on it
wae another on the way

No fur me yer iron tablets
an plenty aw red meat
ma daily dose is Caleys
a keep two at a time at ma feet

The dampness and bad housing
the dugs an lack aw shops
disnae get tae me like it used tae
especially efter six o'clock

A settle doon at ma telly
ma other wee luxury
wae ma five Caleys an ma crisps
a jist melt awae on the settee

Ma wains don't go without
a share everything equallee
they get Caleys fur breakfast
Caleys fur dinner, aye an Caleys fur their tea

I'm no wan fur taking tablets
am sure you will agree
thon wee sweeties wid bend yir head
take a look aroon an see

There's tablets fur sleeping
tablets fur waking
tablets tae make you wee
ony colour you like, frae red an purple
tae blue as the deep blue sea

But not fur me the barbituarites
or anti-depressentees
I'll stick tae ma wee Caleys
but thae don't half make you pee

I'd recommend them tae any wan
they gie you a grand wee sleep
they'r no addictive jist social
an never make you seek

    well that's ma story, sad but true
    ma name will now be known
    it's Kathy the Caley Queen
    an ma life tae you aw I'v shown.

THE CLOSE MOUTH

Weans greeting
Folk meeting
Toilets flushing
Lassies gushing
Wives talking
Men walking
Dogs running
Sills sunning
Middens clattering
Smells battering
Senses thrilling
Stairhead sobbing
Tenements throbbing
Couples winching
Doughballs mincing.
    EAST
    WEST
    NORTH
    SOUTH
All life began at
the close mouth.

A RAP

I'v nae passion fur hoosework
ma lust fur dust is satiated

I'v rested the Domestos R.I.P.
said Sayonari Baby to brill the pad
                        and relatives
curtailed ma kinky nights with the rubbers
                        gloves that is,
I'v skirted the skirting board
and as fur yon unfaithful hoover
well — being — honest it goes fur anything
                        on two feet,

in fact I'm a wummin aw the world noo
outside aw, The Big Clean a mean!

I'v rushed the brush
shooded the loo'ed
beat a path fae the bath
slugged the plug
said nope to sope on a rope

and there's still more to come . . . sure I'v tae

roast the toast
rinse the mince (in arsenic maybe)
mustard the custard
karate the pate
snip the chips
grease the peas
toffee the coffee
and fur ma piece di resistance
I'm gonna vermaccelli his big fat belly . . .

Jane Morris

EAR-PIERCING SCREAMS

"Mum," I said, "does it hurt much?"

"You modern girls are all the same, wanting to be mollycoddled with aspirins and panadols and feminaxes and I don't know what, for the slightest twinge. Of course there's a certain amount of discomfort but it's perfectly bearable. It's a bit late to be thinking of that now, isn't it?"

"That's not fair. There's never been any aspirin in the house, I've just learned not to bother complaining when I have a headache. And I'd have got short shrift from you if I'd dared mention period pains — never a drop of tea or sympathy — I was the only girl in the class who never took a note to be let off gym on account of dysmen."

"Well, you won't get period pains for the next nine months, that's something you can feel grateful for, Jinny."

She can be a cow, my mother. And as the months went on, I became more and more concerned about this question of pain. I thought if I was too much of an ostrich it would take me so much by surprise it could kill me. I went along to some ante-natal classes. We sat on foam mats on the floor of a cellar room in the hospital. There was a dozen or so women, all huge. It was good to blend into the crowd again. The woman next to me was on her third.

"What's it like?" I said.

"Oh, you forget."

"Does this stuff help?"

"Nah, but it's an excuse to come away from the chaos and leave the others with Jim."

We spent a lot of time lying on our backs with our legs up, noticing which parts of our chests were doing the breathing, and feeling perfectly relaxed. It didn't seem terribly realistic to me. The very word "pain" was totally taboo. "Contractions, dear," the woman corrected me. She was clearly a fifty-year-old spinster, and I wondered if she had once taught me hockey.

"Contractions," she repeated, "you can breathe through them, and you probably won't need an injection, at least for the first five or six hours."

Seeing my face, she added, "But if you don't feel you want a *natural* delivery you can always ask for an epidural."

"Sure you can always *ask*, but I never got one," muttered the mother of nearly three.

I knew I'd never ask. The prospect of needles in the spine was worse than the pain, so it would have to be pain and nature. I decided I'd better rehearse a little suffering.

I signed on with a new dentist — after all, it's free when you're pregnant — and he managed to find a cavity that needed filling. I insisted on having it done without an injection. It didn't hurt much, though.

"People make such a fuss about the dentist and there's nothing to it," I told my mother. "Is labour much the same?"

She looked as if I was irredeemably ignorant. "It's entirely different," she said, witheringly.

I continued my quest. I presented myself to a chiropodist and had a corn excavated. This was far worse than the dentist and no anaesthetic was even offered. This was more like it. I gritted my recently filled teeth and cast around for other opportunities to practise bravery.

Walking home one evening I passed a hairdresser which advertised ear-piercing. The boy next door had his left ear pierced three times although his mother walloped him for it. He has tattoos on his arms too. But I digress. This is just one more reason for my mother to despise the poor Pattersons, mother and two sons, who are our neighbours. We don't speak to them but my mother has other, better ways of knowing how far behind they are with the rent, their latest folly on the hire purchase, their emotional escapades.

Mum brought me up to regard ear-piercing as a practice akin to female circumcision, both barbaric and sexist (she regarded Kevin Patterson as the ultimate in perversion and ignored the fact that many young men today sport at least one earring.

"When we were children," she told me, "we begged Granny to let us have our ears pierced. She did Mary's first because she was the oldest and put in her own gold sleepers to keep the holes open. She moistened them with spittle and twisted them round every day. I was so jealous. When I was eleven it was my turn. She did it with a darning needle and a burnt cork."

"Why a burnt cork?"

"Don't interrupt. That's how they did it in those days. Well, two days later I was festering. Both lobes on fire, crimson. They swelled up then broke down and ulcerated. I got such terrible eczema for weeks after. It wept onto the pillowcases at night. I felt like a leper. We had to get the studs out — that was real agony, let me tell you — and eventually the holes closed up."

For weddings and christenings and the big prize night at the bingo, mum wears those things like smarties on clips. They pinch horribly, so by the end of an evening out she'll be nursing them in her lap together with the high-heeled shoes to which she also martyrs herself when she considers the occasion demands it. She's a stoic, my mother. It's not that she thinks you have to suffer to be beautiful. In her philosophy, if you're a woman you have to suffer full stop. And she directs her fury not against the suffering but against any woman who dares complain. Especially me.

Having my ears pierced would admit me to the great company of suffering women, to which my swollen belly even more certainly doomed me. So far things were too good to last — no sickness, no backache, no blood-pressure. I would have to pacify the jealous gods. But I couldn't face that shop. I remembered it as a barber's, although it now called itself Unisex and displayed ear studs on a card in the window, together with a sign saying "No appointment? Come in anyway, we'll fit you in". Any decent place would surely have a queue to the end of the street, and far from an empty appointment book would have a waiting list to rival the NHS. It was a nasty little place; reminded me of a back-street abortionist's. (It was far too late for that, of course.) I was looking for somewhere reassuringly bland and hygienic but neither Boots nor Marks and Spencer pierce ears.

Then, while perusing the knitting wools in Russell's, the poshest of the city's department stores, I spotted a discreet card stating that Mrs Sonia Mobily, Consultant to the House of Fairfax, was available to fit earrings. Her cubicle was half hidden behind the wig department. I lingered a moment among the wigs. My hair seemed adequate but determined sales talk might have persuaded me to prepare for the post-natal fall-out you hear so much about. I saw a pair of agonizingly tight stilettos mince to and fro below the cubicle curtain. I looked in. The other end of Mrs Mobily looked like a free sample from the wig department. She raised one pencilled brow.

She said, "Could you spare us five minutes, madam?"

I could have spared five years to recover from the sight of her holding a metal gun to the head of a young boy. I hoped the perfume department, one floor up, might revive me like smelling salts or possibly numb me like an anaesthetic, and I returned to Mrs Mobily's lair reeking of a mixture of spray samples.

She held the curtain aside and the youth plodded out in his army surplus boots. It was Kevin from next door. Neither of us let a flicker of recognition animate our faces. Such, I imagine, is the etiquette of brothers meeting in a brothel.

"Sorry to keep you," croaked the Madam. "Tricky one that. He wanted it in the cartilage."

I sat on a high, thin stool. The curtain by which I'd entered faced another identical curtain leading to Mrs Mobily's store or smoke room. The other two walls were full-length mirrors, cruel as such things always are when lit by harsh fluorescent tubes. Fortunately the reflections were largely obscured by my bulk and that of Mrs Mobily.

"Nervous?" she grunted at me in such a gruff baritone that I suspected her of being a man in drag but revised my diagnosis to sixty Embassy a day.

"Only a little," I squeaked. Nervous was hardly the word. She wheeled in a small trolley — not a gleaming surgical trolley but a meagre tin tray on castors with some nasty rusty gadgets and a bottle on the top. She took a book of carboned forms from the drawer and I put a tremulous signature to the small print, admitting that I was eighteen or over and disclaiming all rights. I entertained the idea of using a false name but rejected it.

She lifted the gun to my head but before I could scream she lowered it again and held it to the other ear. What was she playing at, Russian roulette? She hadn't pulled the trigger though.

"Your ears are different heights and you have the biggest lobes I've ever come across."

Did she have to get so personal?

"Don't worry about it, everyone's different," she groaned in a tone that implied I was more different than most. Would she refuse to take me on? No such luck. She laid her weapon carefully on the trolley, rummaged in the drawer, found a felt pen and marked two scarlet dots on my ears. I winced.

"Is that alright with you?"

Yes, yes. Far better than holes. I think I'll stay with these painted dots on my ears. Better in every way than earrings. So thank you and good day. But I stayed in my place and nodded fatalistically.

"Which studs do you want?"

"Oh, the gold ones please."

"The young lad just there had my last gold ones, sorry. You can choose from ruby, sapphire or emerald. Simulated of course. But the back parts are gold-plated where they touch your flesh. Guaranteed."

"The blue ones then, please."

"Sapphire. Hoping for a boy then, are you?"

"What? Oh no."

"Doesn't matter which so long as it's alright, eh?"

Actually I was convinced it was a girl and I'd never considered it would be anything but alright. It was me I was afraid for. Like I was afraid right now.

Mrs Mobily tipped some liquid onto a swab of cottonwool so that a gulping sound came from the mouth of the brown glass bottle.

"Spirit," she said. I wasn't sure whether she was exhorting me to courage or describing the fluid.

Before my eyes flashed scenes of it all going wrong, of having to have my ears amputated. I thought of Van Gogh with his bandaged ear. He was mad of course. Well, so was I.

It did hurt, but not as much as I'd expected, not as much as the chiropodist though a bit more than the dentist. Not enough to have got myself so worked up over. It was just two sour nipping pains and then the prolonged expectation that sometime in the next few days I would turn septic.

I didn't get all that drunk afterwards. You're not meant to when you're pregnant, are you? But once I'd started I stayed longer in the pub than I meant. If I went home before mum's bedtime she'd see my simulated sapphires and sniff the cider on my breath.

It was not easy to walk home with both brain and body over-burdened. My efforts were interrupted by a voice from next-door's porch.

"Mrs Day, Mrs Day!"

"*Miss* Day," I replied, shamelessly flaunting my belly.

"*Mrs* Day," she repeated, "could you come in here a moment?"

I hesitated. Then I thought how I'd never been inside that house. I considered how much Mrs Patterson must resent having to ask for help from any member of the Day family. And I remembered how my mother disapproved of us having anything at all to do with the Pattersons. I followed her through the door.

All the houses on our estate are identical but theirs looked as different as possible from ours. I think it was all those tiny china animals on glass shelves. Hundreds of them. All dusted too.

The punk Kevin was sitting at the kitchen table cradling his head in his arms. I thought he might be unconscious from glue-sniffing till I heard curdled sobs. He lifted a swollen red face to stare resentfully at me and then I saw his ear. My hands flew up reflexly to my own ears. The upper part of his left ear was monstrous. Crimson, puffy, weeping — as he was. He looked about four years old and for a moment, in spite of his expression, I wanted to put an arm round his shoulder and croon "There, there now". But Mrs Patterson was glaring at me, arms folded. In a minute she'd clearly be tapping her foot. She was waiting for me to do something. I'd had an education, hadn't I? I was supposed to be able to do things.

"The first thing to do is to get that stud out of his ear."

She shrugged in exasperation. "*You* try then."

The boy sprang out of his chair and backed away, surveying me with suspicion like a wild and wounded animal.

"Sit down Kevin and let the lady take a look at your ear."

I was amazed and humiliated that she called me a lady. I had a good idea what she called me behind my back — that was one reason mum had sent them to Coventry, although *she* called me those same names to my face. I was even more surprised to see Kevin obey his mother. I've never obeyed mine and I'm no punk.

I did my best. I pushed and pulled and probed and tweaked while he said not a word but conveyed by his breathing what exquisite torture I was inflicting. To no avail. And finally he jerked away from me, red-eyed.

"Leave off, can't you," and he buried his head in his arms again.

But I was involved now, and I wasn't going to be beaten.

"Have you tried the doctor?"

"I've no faith in doctors any more. I suppose Dr Beuly wasn't too bad, the one that delivered Kev, but this new one . . . well. I don't hold with women doctors anyway and she's far too young. Refused to deliver Casey at home so I had to go to the hospital. Then last week kicked up a stink about my Valium. I've taken it for years."

"Have you go the number?"

It was one of those plastic pop-up things. The phone was a creepy digital little device with all the business in the hand-set. The idiot doctor was some fool of a night locum. I explained the situation.

"Ho, ho, ho."

Who did he think he was, Santa Claus? When he stopped laughing he said, "My daughter went in for the same crazy stunt. The vital thing is to remove the earring before the whole thing turns septic. Do that and he won't come to grief."

Slam. The phone went dead and I hadn't got a word in edgeways.

"Wanker!" I screamed into the inanimate object, then strode back into the kitchen, feeling aggressive. There was a large fridge-freezer in one corner.

"Give me some ice-cubes," I said.

"We haven't got any," said Mrs Patterson.

Incredulous, I tore open the freezer door. It was crammed with fish fillets in day-glow orange crumbs, and large packets of oven-chips. I took four or five chips from their polythene bag and wedged them around the offending ear, slapping Kevin's hand over them to hold them there. It reduced the swelling, but not enough to allow me to remove the stud. Besides, he wouldn't allow me to touch it for more than a few seconds this time.

"Had I better take him to the Casualty?" suggested Mrs Patterson.

I was humiliated. I was supposed to be the clever one then she comes up with the obvious answer. I said, "If you leave now you should catch a bus, at least one way," and started to button my raincoat, as far as the damn thing *would* button these days.

"Oh, but I couldn't leave the bab," said Mrs Patterson, indignantly. I had forgotten Casey, child of her middle age, and of the rag-and-bone man, if you listened to rumours. Mrs Patterson had after all been married once or twice. I lacked even such retrospective respectability. Be all that as it may, the fact remained that there was a snotty two-year-old snoring up there, preventing them from hopping it to Casualty. I caught mother and son exchanging such shrewd glances I knew I had been set up. They'd never expected me to help, they were merely hunting me down as baby-sitting fodder.

Thirty minutes of uneventful sitting later it dawned on me I didn't know where in the house the baby lay. I heaved my bulk upstairs to locate him in case of emergency. I'd seen him often enough outside the baker's, howling and dribbling soggy biscuit down a blue nylon pram-suit. But he didn't look too bad, sleeping in his cot, sucking his thumb. My heart softened towards babyhood in general.

It was then, leaning against the doorway that a sickening cramp griped at my guts. I shouldn't have gone drinking on an empty stomach. I found the bathroom with haste and sat a while staring at a toilet roll holder in the form of a pink plastic transistor radio. It worked too. It was an interesting bathroom; I remember it well. Frosted shower curtain, crinolined ladies on the wallpaper, foot-crystals, assorted perfumes and talcs, and a loaded medicine cabinet into which I pried shamelessly between pains. I slowly realised that this might be labour; then the possibility turned to panic. I managed to get myself to Casey's cot, snatched him, still sleeping, and somehow reached the phone. After ordering a taxi I carried him, now screaming and struggling with me, to my mother's front door. She met me in curlers, cold cream and quilted housecoat. I pushed the child into her arms. She lifted her reading glasses and her eyes followed me quizzically as I climbed into the taxi and left her.

Well, it *did* hurt. Told you so, I thought, with a certain grim satisfaction as I writhed, grunted and (yes, I admit it) shrieked through the waves of pain. I couldn't "breathe through it" and never even thought to ask for the famous epidural. In less than two hours the small slimy thing was thrust bellowing into my arms and pain and fatigue instantly dissolved into laughter at the expression of outrage on her tiny ancient face.

By dawn, they had bathed us both and we lay decorously side by side in the ward, facing each other across the perspex wall of her hospital crib. I was hypnotised by her perfect sapphire eyes. I had my ears pricked for the sound of breakfast trays but instead heard mum's voice as she argued her way through ranks of orderlies and midwives.

"I'm a working woman, I can't afford to hang about waiting for your proper time. Proper time — stuff and fiddlesticks. I've got bed pans to empty too, you know, and old ladies' kitchens to clean, and shopping to fetch. If you turn me away before I get to see my granddaughter I'll hold you personally responsible for the consequences. I know all the proper channels to complain through, you know."

There was sniggering and one of the girls whispered, "What a character."

Mum sat on the bed and winked at me. "I may be a quaint old Mrs Mop but I get what I want." She laid a packet on the bed and picked the baby out of her cot. "Go on," she told me, poking a finger into the tiny mouth and pulling faces at the baby, "open the box."

There was half a dozen pairs of beautiful earrings in a felt-lined box.

"Your Gran's. I've had them for years. Worth a tidy sum — I had them valued but I couldn't bring myself to part with them, though it seemed a shame none of us could wear them."

I wear them. The ones I wear most are Gran's gold sleepers because when I wear the pretty dangly ones little Harriet laughs and reaches up and pulls hard. That *really* hurts.

TWO POEMS

by Dilys Rose

DREAM FEAST

Like pie-dogs, they cower at the tail end
of every interminable queue, alert to nothing
but the sudden movement of a foot. They pick
and scratch at the periphery, unseeing,
distractedly drawing uncertain circles in the dirt.
They're etched on the scenery. They'll not desert
for richer dunghills but spend a lifetime
praying for windfalls, rotting morsels.
The last lean moon convinced them
they'd be mad to stray. So they linger,
the ugly unlovable glut of dull-eyed waifs
clutching the filthy hem of the world's skirt.

They sleep a lot: their dreams are crammed
with sides of beef, mountains of rice.

TATTOO

He had it done last night:
behind the blinds of Alf's Art Parlour
he scanned the well-thumbed catalogues
until he found an apt motif.

On the left bicep TRUE LOVE presides
on the right a bloody, perforated heart
bruised and dark as a used tea-bag.
Below, a scroll, forget-me-nots

his girl's name etched in curliques.
(It's near as you can get to gold
and guaranteed to come up brilliant
when the scabs have healed).

In the bar, his beer-mates leer
at local girls and tease, 'The lad's
gone daft. It's tax free booze and
hard cash turn them on these days.'

He'd wanted something durable
hit on this hand-tooled brand
He knows that its colours will pale,
its sentiments deepen or fade.

Sheena Blackhall

FLESH AND BLOOD

The holiday brochure lay at an angle, partially obscured by fishing lines and lures. It had been left by the previous occupants of the caravan, folk like Kate and her family with a hankering for the exotic but a purse for the parochial. Its cover was pure Ad-Man hokum, a Mr and Mrs with their two statistically bright, clean, sturdy children, so perfect they could have walked straight off a reel of Nazi propaganda film. The Averages were pictured jetting through the waves, two of life's copers surfing alongside their hygenically tooth-glittering offspring, coyly beckoning the reader into the pages.

Who believed this myth of zestful, family Utopia? The halcyon days of parent-child togetherness? Kate had believed it, not so long ago. . . . The subtle inferences of parents selling the insurance man, foot-in-the-door approach, that children were genetic passports to immortality. The "come on in the water's fine" approach of married peers, who said quite plainly that children were proof of your fertility, fruit of your loins, and dammit, you were born to perpetuate the species — the most gigantic confidence trick of all time. Because children, to Kate, were none of these things. They were a twenty-four-hour job with no chance of promotion, no time off. Nor did you require references to come by them, no aptitude test, or initial screening. They were a play which you created a title for, which then contrarily proceeded to rewrite itself. And you'd never even see the finale, because you'd be dead before the last act.

Brochures should be censored, banned. Brochures were untruths. Holidays en famille were hell.

"I've caught a trout! A trout! Can we eat it now? Please? Please?"

Her son's voice exploded with the violence of a small Hiroshima within the walls of the caravan. Kate shrugged, wearily. Everything had to be now, just when Keith wanted it. Still, his exuberance was almost preferable to his sister's blank inertia. She looked at her little daughter.

Cath sat, a Dresden doll, beautiful, submissive, dense. Kate had so wanted her to be a boy, the old mother-son thing. She'd stared in disbelief at the midwife, holding the wet baby up for approval, new and crumpled.

"It's a girl, dear, a lovely girl."

It couldn't possibly be a girl. Not after so much painful effort. Kate had felt cheated and resentful. Cath was so female, so biddable, so adorable . . . so unwanted. And so consuming. Perversely, sensing rejection, the child clung doggedly to her mother, hungry for attention.

Business kept their father away all day. When he came home, tired and snappish, he would ask accusingly, "Is the racket necessary? Can't a man get any peace? Exert some control, Kate. They are your children, dammit."

For John Neish hated noise. Her children. Never his, only when they were good, which was when they were asleep, or to bolster his macho image before his friends. Then it was "My son Keith . . .".

So Kate would prepare a quick meal, dump Cath in the pram, help Keith on with his wellingtons and walk them around the town, leaving John in possession of his precious quiet.

Keith bullied his sister; despite herself, Kate indulged him. Men were supposed to be masterful. Oddly, the more flaws she discovered in her son, the more she loved him, whereas Cath, so docile, so anxious to please, became more and more of an irritation.

She'd been mending a puncture on Keith's bike last month, one of the 101 jobs that John never seemed to get round to.

"Mummy, Mummy. Come see!" Cath gurgled, from behind the kitchen door. Kate instinctively switched off the request, deaf to all but the immediate issue of the puncture. One thing at a time. Keep calm. The demands were never-ending . . . Cath had gone quiet. She often did, wasn't given to tantrums. She'd learned to suck her thumb and wait. It was what women do best, waiting, getting in the queue behind their brothers.

When Kate finally opened the door, she did so with a long silent scream of revulsion. The toddler's training potty was upturned by the cooker. Cath was smeared in excretia, face, arms, legs. She looked at her mother with a pleasant expression. "Cath painting."

Kate hit her, over and over.

"Dirty bitch. Bloody dirty wee bitch."

She dragged the crying child upstairs, flung her into a bath and scrubbed the filth off, stomach heaving with disgust.

Afterwards, seeing Cath so bewildered and frightened, she'd been sorry. She bought her a toy, a cheap plastic doll. The girl had no way of sensing the deception, that the gift was a guilt token. She'd raised her face for a kiss.

Kate pushed her away.

"Kissing's for babies."

"You kiss Keith."

Keith . . . the trout. Kate's mind refocused on the present. The trout was gulping for breath, a fat shining comma of fright impaled on his hook. Keith hit it; it flopped its tail, and lay inert on the white slab of formica table. Cath began to snivel.

"It didn't hurt you, Keith. You didn't need to kill it. You'll be punished."

Whatever would the girl say next? Kate slit the fish open and gutted it. The salty trout smell rose sharply in the air, a wet smell, an all-pervasive smell. Even as she wiped the knife, it seemed the smell acquired a human element, thick and heavy. Growing and growing, like Gulliver, guilt was squeezing her out. Soon, there would be no space left, the small pocket of identity that had been Kate would be smothered, by flesh and blood.

Sheena Blackhall

COUNT TO TEN

A light shower of rain had drawn the strong smell of trampled grass sharply into the air. Children trickled between amusement arcades, that rose, incongruous as Moslem minarets, on the village green. Garish wooden horses impaled on sugar-stick stands whirled round giggling youngsters, whilst Madame Zsa Zsa, renowned palmist of international repute, slouched against the steps of her caravan, her tight cheap blouse struggling to contain cups of oriental delights which attracted the gaze of beardless boys and red-faced stockmen alike. Men with an eye for beasts admired substantial women. Nearby, housed in a boy scout tent of prim khaki, was "The Smallest Circus on Earth", its carnival fanfare, blaring on a tinny record player, swamped out by skirls from the crowd, as a caber in the Games ring thudded over in perfect style. Admission to "The Smallest Circus on Earth" was 30p.

"Pye us in, ma," chimed two voices, a practised whine.

Their long-suffering parent foresaw, clearer than any palmist, that 60p was a cheap price to pay for ten minutes' peace. She counted the money into a young gypsy's hand, and lit up a cigarette.

"Aren't you coming in too, missis?" he chirped. Libbie Cruikshank glanced into the tent. A handful of bored rodents, ridiculously dressed in Mickey Mouse attire, lounged on Lilliputian swings, or ricocheted round plastic spirals like demented Catherine wheels, depending on their humour, or exciteability.

"I'm waitin' for their da," she said, tersely.

This was not strictly true. Every year, with the fatality of lemmings, the Cruikshank family left their suburban home to visit the Inverithie Games.

For George Cruikshank, it was the binge of the year, a time to huddle tipsily under the marquee tent with kith and kin, drinking deeply of cheap hot whisky from cracked plastic cups and raking over the ashes of old comrades, old courtships.

For Libbie Cruikshank, her outlines billowing with third child, very much enceinte, it was a pilgrimage to Purgatory. It was virtually impossible to keep the children together — they careered skittishly unbiddable from one delight to the next. There were blubbering goldfish in bowls, exotic bearded women, the air a-scream with music, the day filled with flying legs in topsy-turvy milkshake tumbling machines, adrift in the magic of Games Day that hit the community with the force of a flood. Spend, spend, spend; cattlemen and crofters, simpering shopgirls, soldiers, and swaggering teenagers submitting like sheep to the Big Fleece. For once, Scots thrift was given the thumbs down; frippery and flotsam, ephemeral as candy floss whored away their hard-earned pounds in a spree where somehow the tawdriness didn't matter. George Cruikshank, paying London prices for adulterated whisky, would raise not one bleat of complaint, till next day. By then, the Games would be only a sour memory in his mouth.

"The Smallest Circus on Earth" had been a good investment. Ten minutes had come and gone, and the wee buggers were still inside. Libbie indulged in the luxury of a second cigarette, the smoke curled lazily into the sky. Why couldn't her children be content to sit at the ringside watching the *real* Games? Dougal Ban would be competing this year in the heavy events. Dougal, head keeper now on the Inverithie Estates. Dougal, who'd been such a wimp as a boy. God, it was laughable!

Libbie closed her eyes and the Games dissolved around her, like mist. In its place, was a sweet-running burn by a fir wood, and a cluster of woven branches propped up on resinous tree roots, that had been the gang hut.

Dougal Ban would be wearing his kilt and tweed jacket today. Then, he'd been dressed like the other boys, in black shiny leather, à la Elvis Presley, his dark hair combed into a lacquered quiff. The gang had used the hut as a secret den, for smoking, and for the first fumbling lessons in love play. Libbie, gauche and gawky, with no steady beau, had somehow been paired off with Dougal. They had crawled into the darkness of tangled fir like reluctant moles, Dougal, all bravado, but sickly white beneath his acne, Libbie following, a mask of cheap make-up plastered over her insecurity, steeling herself to meet his advances.

They had stared at each other, mutually terrified.

"Ye dinna really want a kiss?" Dougal had asked, hopefully.

"I'm no' bothered," she'd replied, secretly relieved. They'd stayed together just long enough to make it seem as though something had actually happened, before emerging to a gang chorus of wolf whistles.

"Did ye get up tae ten?" asked Neil Rannoch, the gang leader. Libbie affected a blush.

"We got up tae eight," lied Dougal manfully. And then, Libbie really could have kissed him, for saving face. Experience in such matters was calculated by Neil Rannoch on a points system. One was a straightforward no-hands-deviating kiss, two was a love bite, but no one but Rannoch had ever scored the magical ten, though they had only his word he had ever done it at all, with the village daftie at that, an older woman, soft in the head, who was known as the local bicycle.

Libbie opened her eyes, jarred back to the present by a howl from the crowd. Dougal had won a place with the winners. She frowned in recognition at the couple coming towards her. The man was swarthy, with the brown eyes and thick black hair of the hill-bred folk. His wife, a townswoman, was pallid with peroxide tinted perm. Libbie felt a dull flush rise unsolicited from throat to temples. It was Rannoch, now a successful builder, with a sharp city suit and a paunch. She swallowed hard, recalling a Games night in the distant past when, suffused with drink, they had *both* reached the number ten. Crimson with embarrassment, she ducked into the tent.

"Thirty pence, missus!" snapped the gypsy. She fumbled in her purse for the money. The children were poking a white guinea pig. It was either incredibly dead or incredibly tired. Games Day was a goldfish bowl, she reflected. A horrible, horrible goldfish bowl where past and present swam round rogether, forever bumping into each other. Not that that worried George. He'd enjoyed the reputation of being a ladies' man . . . the old double standard. For women, though, morality affected the stance of Australia. It wilfully stood on its head.

The Rannochs had seen her hurried retreat.

"Honest, Mary, I widna touch yon Libbie. She wis jist a bit on the side. Lang ago. A wee hoor."

Libbie's temper flared. For two pins she'd clout Neil Rannoch till his ear dirled. She drew hard on her cigarette. Let it rest. Let it rest. Under currents of old liaisons, like dangerous water, lipped round every Games. In the teen-times of courtship, many couples formed back-of-the-dyke ties that fizzled out like moor-fires when they settled into matrimony with "Mr Right", that figment of Godfrey Winn-type imaginings. There had been George's fling with Mysie Craib, before she had married the butcher from Dunbrae. Libbie was certain that the butcher from Dunbrae added 10p on her bill everytime she shopped at his premises because of it. . . .

Rannoch and his wife were drifting across to the ringside, a dark eddy drawn back into the stream of blood-ties that ran through the veins of the hill-folk, and pulled them like salmon back to their birthplace in this once-yearly Celtic bonanza. The dancers' prizes had been given out. The pipes were droning to a dull deflation. Thank God, it was over for another year.

"Money for the chippie, ma? We could eat a horse!"

Looking into her children's glutinous faces, Libbie could well believe it. With a sigh of resignation, she picked her way fastidiously over squashed beer cans, the day's debauchery dribbling into the turf. George was leaning over the bar, his shirt a fresco of spilled beer and spots of John Begg. He had reached that stage of Scots inebriation bordering on the Bannockburn-cocky, bellicose, and almost legless. Simpering at his side, the spectre at the feast, was Mysie Craib, gazing fondly at him with the look of one who has known him over long, and over well.

Libbie shrugged philosophically.

Count to ten, she thought, count to ten. . . .

TWO POEMS

by Christine McCammond

WELCOME HOME

Christ do I need to talk.
You won't believe what I've been through.
Alex doesn't. Well they don't know, do they?

Six months in a toilet. I kid you not.
Nothing, I mean nothing to do.
He was ok. He had his job, right?

And you know what my nerves are like.
Oh for God's sake, bloody fags.
Can you fix that burn. Not new is it?

Anyway, I just told him.
No money in the world could make me stay.
Jesus, buying a loaf was the day's highlight.

He's been looking for work since we got back.
He'll find something.
Always a good earner, I'll say that much.

I'll never run this place down again.
It's so great to be in civilisation.
The V.C.R. the freezer, everything's just as I left it.

Now if I can unload the dog, I can get into town more.
Do the shops.
Alex says he won't let her go to just anybody. Wants a say in it.

It'll make all the difference. Bloody animals. Worse than kids.
You wouldn't like her? Oh that's alright. Thought I'd ask while I'm
     here.
Anyway, how are you?

A FLOWER FOR WINTER

She gave me plants of fresh green leaves,
Spiky with youth and smelling of life.

No time to refuse, and way too late
For anything to grow.

But I took the shoots and carried them gently,
Swaddling the roots as I would a baby.

They stood in dark earth, raw recruits,
Waiting to be told what to do.

The season changed yet no buds appeared.
High summer saw them clad in fading coats.

On a chill day when silence lay between us like a death,
She walked my garden.

These are gone, I said.
Looking at her gift's decay.

Stooping she reached with a nicotined finger,
And her frailness came at me with a knife, fiercely unexpected.

Just starting, she said.
I gave you autumn crocus, a flower for winter.

Lifting her onto small feet,
I felt bones, brittle as reeds.

For God's sake lose some weight,
I pretended to stagger.

Our laughter sent birds speeding
To their evening tree high above us.

Jane Struth

THE GATE

The morning awoke with difficulty from its grey November cloak
and the woman did not know where she was. Dozens of needling
fingers were poking through cracks in the window and pricked her
bare arms and legs. Shrieks, shouts, thumps and barking assaulted
numb ears, but it was not until the tinny sound of a radio seeped
through the rooms that she realised where she was.

For a brief moment she saw a half-clad deranged-looking woman
lunging along the corridor and making a spectacular entrance in the
kitchen. "Wouldn't it be fun to be mad," she said, as her awful
reflection mimicked the thought.

Suddenly, amidst hugs, kisses and pecks on the cheek everyone but
the dogs were gone and they sighed heavily, curled up on the rug and
resumed their dreams. She surveyed the scene. Last night's supper
dishes, along with spilled cornflakes, the fleshy smell of a half-
consumed tin of dog food, an uncleaned porridge pot and various
other left-around items added to her mounting fear.

Think of Kafka's poor dung beetle suffocating in his dusty
deathbed; think of the order Cezanne would create in one of his still
life paintings. Resolutely she attacked the kitchen.

Looking through the window, she could see the tall dignified shape
of the newly restored cast iron gate shed its ethereal shadow. Its
endurability reassured the woman whose eyes moved slowly up and
down its long vertical bars, lingered lovingly in its circular crevices
and finally rested on the thick solid handle which could now, thanks
to their efforts, turn without the slightest difficulty or sound. A large
part of this area had once belonged to some duke or other but the
nearby mansion and gate were all that remained.

Today I will paint a portrait of the gate, she thought, and her
features began to display their post-morning calm. She began to
collect brushes, paint and cloths, and was about to uncover the blank
canvas when her eye caught today's entry in the kitchen diary. It
simply read — Ann and Bob coming to dinner.

The gate slid behind its shadow. Without looking she knew that the cupboards were bare and all that the fridge contained was a tooth-marked lump of cheese and several half empty wine bottles.

All thoughts of the gate were sucked in by ancient hoover as it groaned and screeched from room to room before finally choking to death on several elastic bands. This seemed a fitting epitaph so she didn't bother to revive him.

The over-stuffed sofa with its gaudy stripped pattern became a pregnant giraffe suckling her bewildered chairs, while the vacant eye of the television stared critically until she flung a dish towel over its awful vision.

Unmade beds exposed their nakedness and she fought back visions of bare white flesh and clothed their recumbency.

Somehow her body did not seem to fit properly into her jeans and there were new alarming lines appearing at either side of her face. I look like a Halloween mask, she thought, and to perfect the image she left her hair uncombed and made towards the village.

In the supermarket rows and rows of shelves displayed packets, tins, and mauled-looking plastic things were being fed by blue and white uniformed girls. "We can't eat these," she laughed aloud and shoved a shopping list at one of the uniforms mumbling something about "dying aunt in hospital" and "can you deliver".

Something beautiful glistened in a shop window and its rainbow colours filled the space. "I'll have half a dozen of these, please," she said and pointed towards the display. When the assistant slapped them down on the cold marble their beauty died and all that remained were several grey trout with glass eyes. She sighed and was about to pay when a large red crab sitting amongst ice cubes began to blow bubbles. "It's alive," she gasped. "Shouldn't be, missus," replied a somewhat confused assistant. "Anyway, yours is dead all right," and he began to serve another innocent customer.

The greengrocer stuffed a selection of vegetables into her basket but she wished that the green stuff sliding down a snotty-nosed child in front of her didn't remind her of boiled cabbage.

Normally the walk back home took only several minutes but her feet involuntarily went the long way round. She came to a halt and gazed somewhat fearfully at the — gate. Feet and trousers were sodden from walking through long grass and her arms felt long and useless. The gate responded to her pull with a reluctant groan.

Lightly — she stepped down the steps, gathering her long skirts as she brushed past the neatly trimmed yew bushes and made her way towards the summerhouse.

Absently — he blew thin whorls of cigar smoke and watched

them disperse one after the other. His long legs were crossed and she could see that he was humming a silent tune for his right foot rhythmically tapped a hidden keyboard.

Silently — they embraced and walked arm in arm through the garden. He plucked a rose and clipped it in her long red hair. She chose a carnation and pinned it to his shirt. They laughed and loved and looked and lingered.

Later — they sipped golden nectar from frosted glasses and agreed that it was the best vintage ever. He raised the glass to marvel at its clarity and her hair glinted red and orange in the sun. When the silent orb slid behind cauliflower trees and small birds ceased their chattering, when the bees hummed their final tune and petals curled in sleep, they too quietly drowsed.

Suddenly a cold fish floundered on to the damp grass and stared wetly at her sodden feet. It looked comfortable lying there so she stepped over it and promptly walked into a dripping towel which was hanging on the washing line.

Mumbling madly to herself the woman unlocked the door and stumbled in.

Propped up against the kitchen table stood a full-length portrait of the gate. The style was unmistakably her own as was the imaginary foliage which crept over and through the delicate fonds. As she stood back to admire the painting a glass shattered. The woman turned to hear the gate click shut and see tiny fragments of frosted glass glisten like rainbow trout as they lay abandoned on the stone steps.

Vivien Adam

OVER MY HEAD

You are the one
He said, over the breakfast
      over my home-baked bread
      over my home-made marmalade
      over my hand-mixed muesli.
      In the attractive container
      A forgotten dried flower.
Who is complaining.
Are we not happy?
I don't really criticize, merely suggest
More organised ways to feather our nest.

      Over my dead body.

I said.

Maree Deeley

NOT LIKE DUCKS

A gauze like film hung over the loch.
Rain fell silently — softly.
Two ducks upturned and disappeared below the
surface, together.
Not like us.

Helen Bell

SLEEPING ALONE

She was dreaming of strange classrooms very lightly when the noise work her up. Fine cold light through the curtains and silence pierced by an animal in pain or maybe courting a mate; an indeterminate animal whose round howls of pain and longing gave it the looks of a large rat with soft cat's paws.

Down below in the garden of the derelict house a ginger dog scraped at a pile of rotting planks, intent on something within. She could see nine slices of garden neatly bricked off into fair shares; on one side a cultivated, crazy-paved piece; in the middle her own, mussed and dotted with plant pots, broken china and a baby bath. Next door the dog stood out from the grey of rotted wood, tree bark and felled branches. He gave up and scampered over a back wall. She watched the pile and waited for something to emerge; the light was pink now and showed heat and sunshine.

"I wouldn't come here if you had rats."

They'd been lying in the dark of his new flat hearing noises you couldn't explain. He'd pushed two single mattresses together on the floor to make his bed. Theirs had been huge with a proper headboard, the gift of a kind neighbour. Stuck to the wood was a scrap of paper with an appropriate quote; his first message to her. The day he moved out she clawed it off and scraped at the shreds of sellotape which stuck there like an empty frame.

The words made her feel stupid.

"Wouldn't you?" His reply was laconic.

"No."

"Why should there be rats? You get rats in places like next door to you."

A nest of pink, blind, baby rats was under that heap. She knew it. A fierce, snarling mother would soon emerge, long and fat as a cat, with rage in its red eyes. Already her ankles tingled and her calves and arms felt exposed to the tearing of claws. She breathed in hard and went back to the bed and made sure the quilt lapped under her feet;

99

no space where a wet black nose could penetrate. She lay quite still, for of course she knew screaming made them worse.

"Come here and look out of the window, pet."

That was her mother calling, twenty or so years ago. The memory was sharp; trotting over to the washing machine and hauling herself up to see. Her mother drained the water from the potato peelings and wiped the knife on her apron then lifted her to look right into the garden.

"Look, see!"

Baby double imperative. Three fat creatures moved slowly up and down on the grass. There was a patch between the house and the hedge about ten yards wide and they crept towards the green shadows and coolness underneath.

"They're water rats. They come from the burn."

Expansion of knowledge, tell them everything. Two were grey-brown, but the most mesmeric was enormous and piebald like a pony in brown and white patches.

She played in a part of the burn which was widened into a pool, deep and brown with minnows, which she tried to catch from a bank of stones and silt. Now among the darting shapes of the fish, she would squint and see something large and powerful move in the dark, peaty water. Then she would throw down the net and scrabble to the road where she could watch through fearful eyes until the memory receded.

With one hand on the dog's collar she would edge forward slowly into the coolness and then dart with her hand to grab the fish. She handed it to her mother.

"They're all dead now pet. They'd never leave oatmeal untouched and it's not as if they can taste the poison."

"Does it hurt?"

"Well, they go back to their nests to die, so they must know they're going to, I suppose."

"Good," she had said.

He stretched and squinted through the shaft of heat, watched the particles of dust move in the yellow slice, and stretched his limbs like a cartwheel. It was still strange to waken alone, but he felt a slow deep pleasure in it. Although she'd slept curled and small her first movement would always be to lie close behind him so that her body imitated his. She could fall asleep again like that, but he needed to move and turn. At first he'd pushed her softly but that had hurt and she'd crawled to the corner and curled against the wall.

"Like a terrapin," he'd thought, and laughed.

Then he'd seen the shoulders shudder and he'd had to give in. Now he couldn't hurt her at all. He had become sick of guilt. Before he fell asleep again he thought of how much he liked sleeping on the floor.

THREE POEMS

by Lindsay McKrell

RESTING

Wrap me round in clean linen
Woollen blankets
Heat my bed
And feed me milk
I have no intention of accepting
The standards you demand of me
You want me bright, precocious,
Well sometimes I am just plain stupid,
Ugly and selfish
I am after all
A gem of many facets
Some of which are dazzling in their brilliance
Some of which are very dull indeed.

I'VE HEARD THIS ONE BEFORE

Oh if you're so Sensual
Why d'you never touch me?
And if you're so Seductive
Why is it my hand on your thigh?
If you're so Sensitive
Why d'you tell me lies?
And if you're so Emotional
Why is it me in tears?

THE SAME OLD SCENE

It's cold in here
Look, you can see my breath in little clouds
Even though the heater's been on hours
Calculating its Easter surprise
Which will probably be prompter
Than the phonecall I'm waiting for, staying in for,
Same old story.
Half of me knows, even as my eyes steal a sneaky glance
at the phone sitting smugly beside me, keeping me company
That it never will ring
It will maintain its stubborn silence
Teaching me a lesson again
Well, that's okay I suppose
I should have known better
But I'd made such plans
Notified friends and neighbours of my new status
Part of a couple again
More of a whole
Than I can be on my own
And I was going to dress up, go out, get drunk,
dance and sing and laugh uproariously
Like I haven't done in such a long time

TOUCHÉ

Deirdre glanced at the mirror. It was just after eight a.m. She could see the cleaner busy at her work, a scarf around her head, her blue checked overall bustling in and out of the partitions, now with disinfectant, next with a mop. It was a relief to feel hot water. She stripped to the waist and washed herself well. She sensed the cleaner eyeing her. She took off her other clothes and finished washing. Hot water lapped her toes. Then she dressed, picked up her luggage, climbed the stairs and stepped into sunshine. Down below, the cleaner took to her cubicle, knitting.

It was quiet in the street. Deirdre sat on her suitcase and let her hair dry. She hung a tea-towel on the railing behind her. Its motif, a scatter of purple-aproned fishwives, announced "Too many cooks spoil the broth" in unobtrusive brown print. Deirdre's hair was drying pleasantly. Runnels of water shone in droplets from its tips, before splashing onto the pavement. She shook it from time to time, enjoying the sun. "Of course," she was thinking, "there should be more nursery schools." That was why she had hung the tea-towel behind her, on the spikes of the public convenience. Across the road dew sparkled on a green triangle. "All the ladies who come here will know they must campaign for nursery schools. They know that, instinctively. My tea-towel will remind them."

As the sun grew stronger, so her hair dried. Deirdre brushed it well, letting the wind curl it and furl it. She felt more composed now, like a bird after preening its feathers. She would sightsee for a while. She was in no hurry to make her journey. Reggie had told her, "Oxford beats with the heart of London, Paris, New York." Bells peeled out of Tom Quad, chiming each quarter. Cobbles pitted her shoes. "On May Day, crowned in white florets, choristers sing from Magdalen Tower, across the Cherwell." She pictured the Meadows, adrift with picnic parties: ladies lolling in the buttercups, attendant esquires, delectables spread on tablecloths, negligent boaters flung like daisies on the grass, punts tied to the bank ready for a leisurely glide back to the boathouse in the early dawn.

She reached her destination, but she had missed the wedding. Louise, in a froth of netting, surrounded by guests who had all given items from the Present List, had been whisked off to her new status. When Deirdre arrived, the marquee was already removed and a mush of lawn remained. Louise's relatives were very kind and made discreet telephone calls. Deirdre stayed the night. The following day she was returned to Oxford.

Dr Dhurnau was attentive. He called to see her every day. She tried to communicate how she was. She talked to him. She wrote reports. She thought of him. He spoke to her from the television screen. It was always his voice, over any other voice, that she heard. She tried very hard to please him. She even witnessed their marriage. As she sat in the stifling lounge, beside the other patients each in her own isolated world, she saw Dr Dhurnau coming out of the church, and she was on his arm. They were smiling and waving. Everyone was throwing rose-petals. A cameraman was snapping pictures at her feet. Dr Dhurnau took her away in a green car.

Louise returned from Switzerland. From the calm of Lac Leman, the splendour of the Vosges and the Jura, her idyllic honeymoon, she now heard of Deirdre's illness. She and Reginald discussed the matter. They phoned the Warneford Hospital and arranged a visit. Louise found Ward V, while her husband waited for her in the car park. Sister Smith unlocked the door and gave her a cup of tea in her office. They watched the patients walk up and down the corridor. The Sister was a very handsome woman. "Ah, yes, Deirdre. A very acute case. Certainly you may speak to her. There she is, over there." Deirdre, her eyes screwed up in the sun, traced a diagonal pattern between the walls, zig-zagging along the corridor. Her arms were stretched out sideways. She looked at the sun through alternate eyelashes. Through the half-opened office door Louise could hear her: "Opalescent, fluorescent, incandescent white light, flame fire, coal forest, burning fire leaves, gone with rapidity, gone forever." She stepped into the corridor. The words were clear: "Catch another fry, friar-bird feather plumed. Flame like hair flows non-stop forever flurry, nothing will avail." Sister Smith called, "Deirdre, you have a visitor. You may take her to your room." Deirdre showed no sign of recognition. Mechanically, she walked to the dormitory. Louise followed.

It was a large room with eight beds in it; a locker stood beside each bed. Deirdre's locker was filled with writings on paper. Conversation was very difficult. Hospital life revolved around meals and drug times. In a locked ward there was little other activity, apart from forced marches into "closed occupational therapy" where egg boxes could be painted in blue, green or red. Louise did not stay long. She was becoming disturbed herself. Reginald gave her hand a sympathetic squeeze as they drove out of the hospital gates.

Sister Furamera was on duty that night. She insisted that Deirdre eat all her jelly and ice-cream. No one was allowed into the dormitories before eight p.m. Everyone was compelled to sit in the sitting room. In this way staff kept patients separate. Diversions could be controlled.

Within the locked ward patients came and went, according to their degree of crisis. Thérèse seemed unable to forget the Maharishi. She had his photo in her wallet. She knew his writings. She felt a cornucopia of love well from his being on behalf of all mankind. She desired to be the instrument whereby his reincarnation would be presented to the world. To achieve that she would have to leave Ward V, and to merit her exit licence she would have to give up her dream. Karen's stay was briefer. She too longed for a child, but was filled with anxiety about having one, as her husband was also her cousin. Pauline was in this ward because her baby had been taken away from her. Her mother would not countenance illegitimacy within the family. Elaine had a habit of slashing her wrists. When Pauline began to imitate her, Elaine was transferred to Broadmoor, a more secure environment. The baby urge affected a nun. Sister Elizabeth became euphoric in her expectations. She bounced from bed to bed, her black gowns flapping in ecstasy. On this occasion Karen joined in, giggling. When Pauline saw two ladies leaping she made a third. Thérèse temporarily forgot the Maharishi and her own weight problems, and added her poundage to the springs. Even Deirdre, distracted from her obsessive interest in her Doctor, jumped from cover to cover. Suddenly all the nurses appeared. They pinned her to a bed at the dormitory entrance. A swift jag and she was out of action. Each patient was caught and quelled. A redistribution of beds within the ward occurred the following day.

Deirdre was now in a dormitory of four. When she was permitted, she joined Marcella and Christine on their sorties to communion in the hospital chapel. A nurse was always in escort, her cape gusting round wintry corners as they dawdled along sanded paths. Marcella talked incessantly of calves, young babies, and milking: to sit on a milking stool, to drink milk fresh from a pail or to churn butter seemed the epitome of happiness. Christine stared with quiet eyes at the white-robed priest, making little distinction between priest and doctor. She liked the chapel, its stained glass and carved misericords, the organ music. It was a change from the ward. A chance also of escaping. In any case, she liked tagging along beside Marcella — who was like a mother to her.

Some months later Reginald drove into the car park. Deirdre saw him drawing up. She was to be allowed out for the afternoon. "We will expect her back for five-thirty, please, Mr Walker." Sister Furamera, her breasts plumped up in her navy uniform, beamed goodbye. Deirdre heard the door lock behind her. They walked along miles of corridor and stairways and finally reached fresh air. It was springtime. "I thought you might like a drive," suggested Reginald. "Oh, Reggie," smiled Deirdre. "You know me inside out."

She felt glad to see rolling countryside, villages and fields. They wandered round a ruined abbey. "How about tea?" Reggie chose a small hotel which also served afternoon teas. "It's something we in Britain do particularly well." They ordered a pot of tea and toasted tea-cakes. Shakily Deridre poured. Reginald noticed a gleam of firelight on her hair, its glinting burnished on the copperwork in the hotel drawing room. Her skin was rosy with fresh air and flame. "I'll tell Louise how well you look." Deirdre blushed. "She'll think you're a pig, you taking me out and not letting her come too." "Oh Louise is far too busy polishing the family silver. We're having rather a special guest this weekend." They turned into the Warneford gates as the hospital clock sound the half-hour. Reggie kissed her lightly outside Ward V, and then pressed the bell. Sister Furamera was breathless. She was in the middle of serving the meal. However, Deirdre's sausage and mash were in the hotplate. The dressing down was not severe.

Dr Dhurnau too was pleased with Deirdre's progress; besides, he wanted her bed. She was now permitted to go to the ordinary occupational therapy — always accompanied, with other patients from the "closed" ward. They joined in discussions and debates, stuck mosaics on bottles, played darts and table tennis. More importantly, she met William. He was a "school refuser" from the Adolescent Unit. He could come and see her in her ward at the correct visiting times, and they were allowed out in the hospital grounds together. They stared at cattle on the hospital farm. They ploughed through mud, their shoes ankle-deep in it, relishing its squelch and smell. Young companions, they sported together. "Words are a net," pronounced William, "through which meaning escapes. I fish for silence." With such profundities they passed the time.

It was early summer. Reginald returned. "D'you remember the 'special visitor' I mentioned the last time I was here?" Deirdre was listening. "Well, that was your doctor. He wanted to see if we could provide you with 'after-care' in a 'stable environment'. Louise and I thought we might set up a ménage à trois, if you agree. She's expecting our first baby. I didn't tell you. It was after she came to see you. That scene, her description, it was so traumatic. You could give her a hand. It'll be a step towards that nursery school idea of yours. What d'you say?"

"It's very kind of you."

"You're not going to be churlish? You're not going to refuse?"

"I can hardly say no, not with a baby due."

"What'll I tell Louise?"

"Say yes. Tell her I'll not let her down. I'll make up for not being at the wedding. I'll clean the silver. But please, please invite Dr Dhurnau to dinner — perhaps on Midsummer's Eve, when the honeysuckle is out."

"Rupert is emigrating, Deirdre. He's taking Jacquie and young Thomas with him. Their next child will be born holding a maple leaf. You knew he had a wife, didn't you?"

"Yes, but I thought I was the one he married."

"You silly goose. That's 'transference' for you. Jacquie is a physio, at the General. Now don't give Louise weird ideas about us, will you?"

Louise opened the door. Her smile was a wide as the torta she produced at the end of a candlelit dinner. Rotundity suited her. She rested after the meal. Reginald and Deirdre cleared the table. Deirdre washed up. Reginald dried the dishes. He showed her where everything lived. Louise settled onto her piano stool, lost in an Appassionata. Reggie grinned at Deirdre behind Louise's upright back. At the conclusion of her last rapturous Divertimento, their applause was cordial.

Gillean Somerville

JAMILA'S WEDDING

For Hamid and his family in Fes, with love and thanks.

"In 1890 Dr J. G. Frazer, in his monumental work *The Golden Bough* (second edition, 1900), . . . referred to the existence of a mass of facts showing that the origin of the marriage system was to be found in some primitive conception of danger attaching to the sexual act."

     A. E. Crawley, *The Mystic Rose*, Spring Books, London, 1965. (Modern reprint. First published by Macmillan, London, 1902.)

"In Morocco, at the feast before the marriage, the bride and groom sit together on a sort of throne; all the time the poor bride's eyes are firmly closed, and she sits amid the revelry as immovable as a statue. On the next day is the marriage. She is conducted after dark to her future home, accompanied by a crowd with lanterns and candles. She is led with closed eyes along the street by two relatives, each holding one of her hands. 'Such is the regard to propriety on this solemn occasion, that the bride's head is held in its proper position by a female relative who walks behind her.' She wears a veil, and is not allowed to open her eyes until she is set on the bridal bed with a girl friend beside her."

     A. R. Crawley, ibid.

"In Western culture, sexual inequality is based on belief in women's biological inferiority. This explains some aspects of Western women's liberation movements, such as that they are almost always led by women, that their effect is often very superficial, and that they have not yet succeeded in significantly changing the male-female dynamics in that culture. In Islam there is no such belief in female inferiority. On the contrary, the whole system is based on the assumption that women are powerful and dangerous beings. All sexual institutions (polygamy, repudiation, sexual segregations, etc.)

can be perceived as a strategy for containing their power.... At stake in Muslim society is not the emancipation of women (if that means only equality with men), but the fate of the heterosexual unit...."

Fatima Mernissi, *Beyond the Veil, Male-Female Dynamics in Muslim Society*, Al Saqi Books, London, 1985.

Fes, September 1985

Aziz leans on the rooftop parapet in the sun. A sound of frantic scuffling disturbs the quiet. In the unpaved street below several barefoot boys in grubby shorts and torn jerseys are chasing a football. To and fro, pounding the dry beaten earth, pass, dribble, feint and tackle, collision and plaintive argument. There is no referee to resolve the squabbles. Aziz regards them with detachment. His own ambitions in that line are long dead. Once it might have offered a way out, but there are so many undiscovered Maradonas of the back streets. He flicks a tail of ash from his Marlboro and observes its descent down the outside wall of the house. Boredom is an established feature of his life.

A light wind whips through the heat. The hem of his black cotton gandoura lifts and swells. He clutches it, as a woman might, trying to preserve her decency. He scowls, screwing up his eyes against the sunlight. He needs glasses. He cannot afford either the treatment or the cure.

Into this suspended moment the music leaped. The first note rang out like the muezzin's sonorous call to prayer, with which I momentarily confused it, but in an instant we were overwhelmed by an altogether wilder sound, swelling up from the bowels of the house, pulsing and pounding like the war drums of the black tribes of Africa, compelling attention and even invoking fear.

"What is it?" I ask.

"Is the women."

"But what are they *doing*, for heaven's sake?"

"Is for the marriage. Is always the same."

"But Jamila's wedding isn't until Saturday. Days away. Does this go on all the time?"

Aziz preserves his laconic indifference.

"You will see with your own eyes."

And hear with my own ears, too, evidently.

It annoyed me at first, like a "ghetto-blaster" turned up full pitch.

But, bit by bit, I found myself surrendering to its weirdly hypnotic spell. The women, assembled together in the sitting-room, beat goatskin tambourines in a vigorous rhythm and then raise their voices in a harsh incantatory chorus. Sometimes a solo voice will detach itself, soaring on tremulous wings, carrying the song to perilous heights, then, its improvisation exhausted, will blend back into the raucous chorus again. When the chorus, too, finally fades, the women hold the tambourines high above their heads and beat out a thunderous, climactic tattoo, which falls at last like waves against a prolonged electric outburst of those high-pitched, piercing cries, known as *les you-yous*, the quivering ululations of joy with which the women celebrate a happy occasion.

These are not the coy seductive cadences we might more readily associate with the harem. This is strident and unearthly. With it the women support and sustain the bride through her approaching time of trial and danger, scaring jealous spirits, dispelling the evil eye and doubtless cleaning their own souls of whatever tensions and frustrations may afflict them.

Three days later. Wednesday. Today is cake-baking day.

After lunch the women clear the downstairs sitting-room. The cushioned divans which normally run along each wall, defining the social space, are piled up at one end, as if for a removal. The television, draped in its muslin cloth, has been removed to the store-room behind the shop, together with the Spanish flamenco doll who flaunts her layers of turquoise satin upon it, the framed colour photograph of the last family wedding and the calendar whose date is never altered from week to week, or even month to month. The green and white tiled floor is swept and wiped over. One of the girls will take hold of a damp cloth the length of a towel, one end in each hand, and then, keeping her feet about eighteen inches apart and her knees straight, will move rapidly backwards, rubbing the cloth to and fro against the tiled surface.

A dozen long metal baking trays, buckled out of true by continual exposure to intense heat, lean against the wall by the front door. The girls wash them down with a solution of Tide mixture with water from the downstairs tap. Huge, brightly coloured, plastic tubs, each large enough to bath a miner in, are set out in the middle of the floor. Both trays and tubs have been borrowed for the occasion. The packages of ingredients are then heaped up beside the tubs.

Mou Aîcha, Aziz's mother, spreads blankets on the floor for us to sit on. The front door has been left open. Outside the street is empty.

The shops are closed. It is siesta time. A light breeze ruffles the transparent curtain that hangs across the doorway. There is little light, except for the doorway and two tiny square apertures high up in the wall. An Arab house closes in on itself. Flies buzz. Fatima sprays the room with insect repellant, drenching us in a sickly sweet odour which brings tears to our eyes and makes us cough, but has no effect on the flies. Upstairs Aziz and his father take their customary post-prandial nap.

"Why are we waiting?"

"For the women," replies Suraaya cryptically as she pounds freshly peeled almonds in a mortar for marzipan paste.

As the family's only university student, Suraaya has been allocated to me as guide and interpreter when Aziz is otherwise occupied. I feel she resents my alien curiosity. I am an outsider.

Mou Aîcha sits cross-legged and silent, the restlessness of her cheek muscles betraying her inner anxiety. In my experience Mou Aîcha is always anxious. She tends to show her emotions. She is in her late fifties, small, plump and although strong often unwell. She has had no formal education, cannot read or write and has never worked outside her home. She and her husband, Ba Abdullah, have brought up eight children. There was also one who died. She presides over her family's tribulations with a compassionate pragmatism. Her compassion makes it harder. Her children are devoted to her. She is their abiding source of emotional strength. She asks little of life, except health and strength, her children's happiness and enough money to get by. But God's ways are mysterious and troubles come frequently. Her powers of resignation are sorely tried. *"Muktub"* — It is written.

Jamila, Suraaya and Fatima are her three remaining unmarried daughters. All three are attractive, lean and fine-boned, with that distinctive bloom of youth. Jamila has woven rugs in a craft workshop in Fes's Ville Nouvelle since the age of eight. Education is still not compulsory in Morocco and Jamila's lack of progress at elementary school, coupled with the family's poverty, made her parents decide that she would be better employed learning a trade. Fatima has finished elementary school and now helps her mother in the house. Although Jamila and Suraaya wear European clothes to work and university, at home they wear traditional Moroccan dress. Their long shiny black hair is always plaited and hidden under cotton headsquares knotted on top of their heads. They dress like this from choice, not compulsion. They feel more comfortable conforming to the habits of their family and neighbours. Outside they wear colourful silk djellabahs. They wear no make-up, except kohl to freshen their eyes. Make-up is frowned on, is not respectable. They exude an aura of unblemished femininity, carefully nurtured in a sheltered place, and finding them husbands is a necessary consideration. It is a disgrace for a girl not to marry. Marriages are often arranged, frequently between cousins. Courtships are conducted with decorum and under supervision. Parents agree the terms of the marriage contract.

As far as one can tell, Jamila's engagement is a love match. Her fiancé, Abdeslame, is a metal-engraver in the same craft-workshop. Today she sits quietly by herself on a low stool, not joining in the wedding preparations, as is her privilege, but she looks far from happy. A bad attack of wedding nerves, perhaps? Normally a lively mischievous girl, she now looks listless and preoccupied. She is also fasting this week to make up for the time lost during Ramadan because of her period. From being, from my point of view, enviably slim, she has become worryingly thin.

Shortly before three o'clock a shadow falls across the doorway and a hand draws back the curtain. Merriem has arrived with her two little girls. The eldest of Aziz's sisters, she lives with her carpenter husband, Ibrahim, in a two-room flat at the back of a large apartment block in the Ville Nouvelle, servants' quarters from the days of the French Protectorate. She is heavily pregnant with her third child. She is praying for a boy this time, a woman's only hope of comfort and security in her old age. She is wearing a black polo neck sweater under a long pale pink broderie anglaise dress. She moves slowly about the room, bestowing her greetings. The little girls dart about like fish in a pond, rushing in and out of the house, wanting to play in the street that is coming alive again, but not wanting to miss a trick inside either.

Merriem's presence heralds the arrival of the other women, friends and neighbours, who have come to help bake the wedding cakes. Soon the room is crowded and awash with women's voices. Cheeks are conscientiously kissed, evil ritually expelled, djellabahs unzipped, peeled off and thrown over the heaped-up divans. Babies are unslung from the towels which secure them to their mothers' backs and deposited in their nappies on the floor, whimpering a little, their eyes wide with apprehension above the huge plastic pacifiers thrust into their mouths. Then the women roll up their sleeves, securing them with a circle of elastic which they twist crosswise over their breasts. The hems of their long skirts are tucked into their waistbands, leaving their ankle-length drawers exposed. Thus accoutred, they set to work.

A large mountain of a woman called Doha takes charge. Her energy quite undiminished by her Rubenesque proportions, she kneels ceremoniously by the central orange tub and supervises the wholesale inpouring of flour and sugar, raisins, almonds and walnuts, yeast powder and vanilla flavouring and an explosive cracking of eggs. Then, with a confident flourish of her fleshy arms and strong wrists, she mixes the ingredients by hand. A thorough, glorious squelch.

The end product of this communal exercise is not a single wedding cake, but lots and lots of tiny spiced confections. The chief of these, and the ones for which the highest skill is reserved, are the *cornes de gazelle*. This again is Doha's speciality. She and a friend sit cross-legged on the floor facing each other across a low, round table on which they pound balls of white puffy dough. The dough is then rolled out until it is very thin and as light and elastic as a baby's vest. Small strips of marzipan paste are then encased in sections of the pastry, the edges crimped together and the final shape bent into that of a new moon. This precise work takes hours. The women's fingers move swiftly and deftly. The continual gossip is interwoven with snatches of spontaneous song. When the trays are full they are taken to the local baker's oven to be cooked.

It is nearly eight o'clock in the evening before the whole process is finished. The cakes, still warm from the oven, are checked before being packed in cardboard boxes and hidden away until the wedding day. Mou Aîcha is disappointed with one set, Swiss roll lengths of biscuity texture with currants which have to be sliced and which crumble away as she does so. Too many eggs? Too hot an oven? The *cornes de gazelle*, however, are pronounced a triumph. The women sample their efforts upstairs in the smarter sitting-room, washed down with hot sweet mint tea.

In the old days Moroccan brides were fattened for their weddings. Whether this was for aesthetic reasons or a subtle form of social control, I don't know. In a poor country being fat tends to be perceived as a sign of wealth and is in consequence rare. Jamila indicates that she would like to swop her thinness for my *embonpoint*. We giggle over this. If only it were possible.

She shows me her trousseau — a white and brightly patterned silk kaftan, a white silk djellabah, white cotton headsquares and beige suede slippers embroidered with gold thread. The clothes are all hand-stitched, made by craftsmen in the workshop in the Ville Nouvelle. She also proudly shows me her cosmetics with which she will be made up on her wedding day. Jamila is fashion conscious, loves clothes and artistic display, far beyond her means. This trousseau has been paid for by Abdeslame as part of the bride price agreed many months before between both sets of parents. The clothes have been folded away in a leather suitcase until they are ready to be worn.

Merriem's present to the bridal couple is a set of hand-embroidered sheets, pillowcases and bolster cover. She has been working on it for months and is now on the second pillowcase. It must be ready to be taken to Jamila's new home, with her parents-in-law, on Friday afternoon. The exquisitely fine stitching demands total concentration. The pattern is worked entirely in dark blue thread. Along the edge of the material is a geometrical design of symmetrical triangles, each side of which is spiked with rows of tiny hooks as delicate as lace. From these rigid mathematics blossom tiny flowers, each stitch curved and looped to suggest growth and grace. The centre of the material is filled with flower shapes as intricate and regular as snowflakes. Each thread of the material is counted, she tells me.

This evening she is tired. She stretches out her legs on a divan and supports her back against a pile of cushions. Her ankles are swollen. She complains of the pain. I tell her she needs help. She says she has no one, one of the perils of not living with one's extended family. Behind her present fatigue lies the shadow of a more settled depression. Merriem would like to be comfortably off, but Ibrahim earns very little and her whole life is a continual scrimping and saving to make ends meet. She supplements Ibrahim's wage by embroidering sheets and pillowcases for the weddings of friends and acquaintances, but as well as being time consuming, dreary and repetitive, it is hard on the eyes. She would be better with a machine, she tells me, but that is beyond her means.

Suraaya keeps a careful record of all the wedding presents. This is necessary as the family's debt to friends and relatives. In due course a reciprocal gift will be expected at an appropriate time and woe betide if you forget. Moroccans have long memories for such transactions. Every so often Suraaya reads out the inventory to remind her mother what the score is.

On the day before her wedding a Moroccan bride undergoes two important rituals. The first of these is the visit to the *hammam*, or public steam bath.

Like many traditional Arab households, particularly of the poorer sort, Aziz's family do not possess a bathroom. Instead everyone goes to the local *hammam* at least once a week. It's an elaborate ritual, certainly for the women, by the side of which a daily bath or shower is seen as absurdly inadequate.

The women's *hammams* I have visited cocoon you in a woman's world as securely as in a convent. In a bare, functional reception area you strip to the skin and make your way barefoot through windowless, steaming halls, littered with scraps of orange peel and discarded hair. A shrill cacophany of sound explodes around you, as in any swimming pool, echoing the sharp accents of animated female discourse. In a pall of steam women of all ages, shapes and sizes sit like priestesses, combing out their long black glossy hair with rhythmic strokes and guarding their personal allocations of hot and cold water, which you collect yourself in plastic buckets from a stone cistern, like lynxes. Bodies bulge with Buddha-like amplitude, displaying here and there the ghost white scars of a Caesarian section.

The ease of their nakedness impressed me. Outside they spend their whole lives swathed from head to foot. The older and orthodoxly religious women wear veils. Only a minority, and those chiefly the well-to-do, habitually wear European clothes. In the seclusion of the *hammam*, however, they seem able to throw off this shrouded conformity, to relax and be themselves.

On this particular occasion Jamila puts on her white silk djellabah and white headsquare for the first time. Fatima takes tea and cakes to the women who supervise the *hammam* to warn them that a bride is on her way. The money for the afternoon's ablutions arrives from Abdeslame. To a tumult of chants, ululations and beating of tambourines, Jamila leaves the house, accompanied by her sisters and friends. All the neighbourhood must be kept informed.

The same celebrations greet Jamila's return some three hours later. She is taken upstairs to rest and recover. A visit to the *hammam* must be treated with respect. Her friends and sisters sing the wedding songs they find it difficult to translate for me:

> "You are like a bird on a staircase, poised for flight, impatient to spread your wings and fly away. What shall I do without you, O my daughter? How shall I live on here, all alone, bereft?"

And Jamila weeps silently from the emotion of the occasion.

The second ritual is that of the henna. It takes place in the evening and could be regarded as the first formal social event of the wedding. Guests start arriving about seven, mainly women, smartly dressed in exotic and colourful kaftans, probably bought new for the occasion. At one end of the sitting-room sits a beleaguered and depleted tribe of men — Aziz, Ibrahim, Abdeslame, the husbands of a few of the women guests. They will preserve an attitude of disinterested observation throughout the evening, sharing out their Marlboros and talking among themselves. On this occasion there was no stag night. Whether this is common, I don't know. Perhaps male bonding is less threatened by marriage here. Ba Abdullah keeps well out of the way. It is not seemly, apparently, for the bride's father to participate in the wedding celebrations.

In a side room the redoubtable Doha, wearing an apricot kaftan and a pink headsquare, is testing the consistency of the henna paste. Fatima bought the dried leaves in the *soukh* that morning and later ground them into a powder. The powder was then mixed with hot water to make a creamy texture, dark green, almost black, in colour. When Doha is satisfied she takes the bowl of paste through to the sitting-room where Jamila is waiting, bolstered with a pile of cushions. The ceremony is ready to begin.

Outside the night is hot and sultry. The high sitting-room windows are, exceptionally, left open. The women raise their tambourines and begin to sing another wedding chorus.

Henna is considered to have magical properties. Pregnant women as well as brides hope to ward off the evil eye by its application. Merriem's hands show traces of it. Resting her arms on a cushion covered with an embroidered cloth, Jamila stretches out her hands with their long thin fingers and Doha settles to her task. Like Merriem's embroidery the application of the henna is an exacting process. The paste is drawn from the bowl on the end of a small wooden stick, much like an orange stick, and not so much painted on the skin as laid across it in tiny lengths, perhaps a centimetre at a time. The delicacy of the design likewise recalls the embroidery, displaying a similar blend of the floral and the geometric. The hands alone take Doha two hours. When they are finished they give the impression of wearing a pair of very fine black lace gloves.

Although it is a long session, Jamila seems to have recovered her usual impish good humour for the occasion. This is no doubt enhanced by Abdeslame's presence in the room, his first appearance in the house all week. "He has many things to arrange," Aziz explains, but this for me emphasises the priority of the tribal over the personal in such a wedding. Abdeslame is a small, stocky man in his twenties, with a round open face, an agreeable grin and a tight bristly crewcut. Jamila's flirtatious tendencies are oblique rather than direct. Open flirtation is frowned on. Instead, there is much irrepressible giggling with her girlfriends between the choruses, rising to a pitch of hilarity during the break for supper when Jamila, her hands out of commission, has to be fed like an invalid.

After supper it is the turn of Jamila's feet to be hennaed. This, too, takes a couple of hours. After the henna has been applied it has to dry. Jamila warms her hands and then her feet over a small metal charcoal burner which has been sprinkled with incense. Then her hands and feet are tied into white cotton bags so that she can sleep without spoiling the pattern. In the morning the black strips of henna will be removed with cottonwool soaked in warm water, leaving the lacy pattern stained a delicate brick red.

It is midnight before Doha finishes with the bride. Then Abdeslame is summoned to receive some solid macho blobs in the palms of his hands. Then it's a free for all for those who wish to receive some of the henna themselves and those who want to show off their skill in its application. Doha disappears to wash her hands, wipe her brow and take a well-earned rest. A tall phallic cone of solid sugar wrapped in blue paper stands on the table beside the charcoal burner as part payment for her labour.

It has been a good evening. The singers are hoarse and exhausted. One by one the windows are closed and the guests disperse. It is after two o'clock before the family is in bed.

In spite of the late night, everyone is up early on the wedding morning. The quiet rooftop, traditionally the place where the women do the family washing and take exercise in relative privacy, hums with activity. Fatima sweeps away the dust and throws bucketfuls of water over the concrete expanse, streaming into the central drain. Suraaya and some other young girls from the neighbourhood lug wooden divan bases and cushions up the narrow concrete staircase from the ground floor. Many of these, too, have been borrowed. The divans are set out round the perimeter of the rooftop and light metal chairs in one corner for the band. The brieze block walls of the parapet are hung with tapestry pictures and tinsel streamers. Aziz's younger brothers, Kemal and Karim, shin up and down the parapet and on to the corrugated iron roof of the store-room, fitting a large borrowed tarpaulin to shade the guests from the sun. Aziz helps rig up an electric light bulb circuit to illuminate the festivities after dark. A "throne" for the bride and bridegroom is built out of metal chairs piled high with cushions on top of one of the divans and then concealed under the smartest of the divan drapes. A Moroccan wedding is an occasion for display. "If we are more rich," Aziz says, "everything would be more nicer." His family does what they can with what they have.

Downstairs Mou Aîcha and a group of women neighbours are sitting cross-legged on the floor plucking chickens. Mou Aîcha went shopping in the *soukh* first thing and brought back twelve freshly slaughtered and bloodied carcases in her bag. Guts and white feathers fly from their fingers and blood strains across the tiled floor. With a pot of boiling water they make short work of the task. They are not squeamish, these women. The circumstances of their lives forbid such self-conscious responses.

By lunchtime the rooftop is ready for the reception of the guests. The heat intensifies. Downstairs a huge plastic barrel is filled with cold water. The fridge is packed with coca cola and mineral water bottles of tap water to be chilled. The water supply is cut off every evening at five o'clock, but the guests will be thirsty and so an adequate supply must be drawn off now. I splash some water from the rooftop tap on to my arms and the back of my neck. The coolness is like champagne, one drink which will not be in evidence at this wedding.

About midday another outburst of ululations and beating of tambourines marks Jamila's return from having herself made up for the wedding. She strikes me as looking frail and vulnerable, standing there in the dimly lit room, the centre of admiring attention, wearing a long pale shift, chaste as a nun's. Her broad smile looks strangely masklike and insecure. The wedding make-up is elaborate. Her jet black hair is piled on top of her head like a crown and decorated with tiny pearls and white artificial flowers. Her eyes are shaded violet, her eyelashes thickly mascaraed, her cheeks vividly rouged and sprinkled with miniature pearlised stars. On her hands, her wrists, in her ears and round her neck she wears the sum total of her worldly wealth — her wedding ring, a gold bangle, gold earrings and a gold pendant in the form of a miniature *porte-korane*. Her hands and heels show the red tracery of the henna. On her feet are the suede slippers embroidered with bold thread. She is greeted by everyone in the traditional manner: "Saleim erroussa" — Peace to the bride.

After lunch the cakes are unwrapped and heaped up on the large round ceramic plates from which they will be served. Muslin cloths are laid over them to keep the flies at bay. Mou Aîcha's forehead is etched with anxiety, but the troops are in order, her girls well trained, the logistics carefully calculated. The general need have no worries.

The all-male band arrives, clattering briskly up the stairs with their instruments and music stands. There are drums, violins, flutes and tambourines, also a singer. Hot on their heels come the first of the women guests in colourful kaftans that swirl about them as they walk. Fatima and Suraaya show them up to the rooftop and bring them glasses of chilled water. The band tunes up and tries out a few warm-up numbers. It is like the opening night of a theatre drama. All those months of anxious preparation and now the moment of truth.

From the street comes the penetrating chant of a new set of female voices. Invoking the blessings of Allah, these are the *ngefat* come to dress the bride. These are women whose business it is to display the bride in a sequence of traditional wedding costumes hired for the occasion. They may be in business for themselves or they may work for someone else. They provide a service for brides who cannot afford to provide such clothes for themselves. They arrive carrying large bundles knotted on top of their heads and one had what looks like a gigantic wooden tray, as big as a cartwheel and painted in bright flower patterns. Jamila goes to sit with them in a room apart.

Although I would prefer to remain in the background I am continually thrust forward to be introduced. All the guests seem curious about me. Few of them have met many Europeans and those most likely to be French. Where I come from is only of marginal interest. *L'Ecosse* is easily confounded with *La Corse* and both might be situated east of Cairo. What matters is that I am European and a friend of the bride's family. They also persuade me to join in the dancing. It is no small miracle I can find some rhythm of my own to respond to their more seductive one. People thrust five-dirham notes into the waistband of my skirt and the neck of my T-shirt. Disconcerting as this is, I am assured it is a gesture of appreciation. The money, however, is for the band.

There is a curious ambivalence about the dancing. To my eyes undeniably erotic, the dancers' movements seem held in check by a determined refusal to acknowledge that eroticism. There is no alcohol to release inhibitions. No one behaves flirtatiously. And yet people dance as if they're thoroughly enjoying themselves.

Just as an atmosphere of cheerful relaxation sets in, the dry tuneless chant of the *ngefat* rises from the staircase. The band slurs to a full stop. The *ngefat* emerge on the rooftop leading Jamila by the hand wearing the first of the four costumes in which she will be displayed during the course of the afternoon. Over her own white, claret and beige silk kaftan she is swathed in a robe of magenta silk embroidered with gold flowers and trimmed with gold thread. On her head is a high gold crown, fashioned like the walls of an ancient city, encrusted with jewels. Cascades of pearls and gold hang down either side of her head, strings of pearls around her neck. The *ngefat* help her on to her "throne", invoke the blessings of Allah on her and her marriage and then leave her, her gorgeous skirt spreads out around her, alone, motionless, unsmiling, her eyes fixed on a far distance. For more than an hour she sits like this while the band plays, the young guests dance and the rooftop is packed to capacity. Mint tea and cakes are served. So is chilled water. People fan themselves with whatever they have to hand.

At sunset Abdeslame arrives with his friends. He is wearing a smart new pale grey linen suit and an open-necked white shirt. They sit together in one corner away from the bride. Two of the *ngefat*, flanking the bride, declare to the assembled company that they are holding her hostage and only a ransom payment can release her to her husband. One by one the guests queue up to kiss the bride on both cheeks and to put a tip in a bowl held by one of the *ngefat*. This done, the *ngefat* satisfied, Jamila is pronounced "ransomed" and Abdeslame is allowed at last to join her.

In her second transformation Jamila appears encased in a rigid frame covered with green, white and gold striped brocade. The frame is a large half moon shape. On her breast she wears an elaborate bib of targe-like silver pendants each set with a turquoise stone. This time the *ngefat* roll up the wooden tray in which Jamila is placed cross-legged. The *ngefat* then raise the "tray" to their shoulders and to the accompaniment of a thunderous clapping, chanting and beating of drums, twirl her round and round above the heads of the guests. Then it's Abdeslame's turn. He clowns a bit, obviously feeling self-conscious, but prepared to go through with it for the sake of the occasion with his customary good humour.

For her third transformation Jamila wears her own white, orange and turquoise kaftan, over which the *ngefat* wind a toga of gold silk. On her head they place a pearl tiara.

In all these costumes Jamila preserves a resolutely serious remoteness. In her final transformation, however, she is dressed like a Berber girl from the Rif Mountains, and with Abdeslame clothed in a corresponding turban, djellabah and yellow leather *babouches*, they were allowed to join freely in the dancing. Later she told me that this was her favourite of the four costumes. She wore a long white dress drawn in at the waist, from which hung two loops of navy tinsel. Round her neck she wore silver Berber pendants set with red and green gemstones. Her head was covered with a black cotton headsquare, from which a row of coins, attached by coloured threads, hung across her forehead.

The wild, enthusiastic Berber dance proves to be the climax of the afternoon's ceremony. It is now eight o'clock in the evening. The band packs up and departs. The last of the official photographs are taken. Jamila is disrobed and the *ngefat* depart with their bundles and the "tray", still sternly chanting. The guests who have not been invited to stay also depart. So, surprisingly, do Abdeslame and his friends. They have to prepare for Jamila's reception at her new home later that night.

There have been no legal, nor, apart from the invocations of the *ngefat*, religious aspects to this ceremony. The official papers have all been signed months before. The public ceremony is quite separate and entirely voluntary.

We eat and then we wait.

Up on the rooftop the night is now pitch black and at last gratefully cool. There is space to breathe also. Some of the young girls of the neighbourhood want to talk to me. What are weddings like in Europe? Why amn't I married? In Morocco it would be a great dishonour for a woman not to be married at my age. I refuse to be disconcerted. In our culture, I explain, women have more independence now and more freedom of choice. You don't have to marry if you don't want to, or if no one suitable turns up. But still most women prefer to marry. They are obviously very intelligent, some of these girls, but they have had little education beyond elementary school and their lives are restricted to helping their mothers at home until an acceptable husband comes along to deliver them from one form of bondage to another. Marriage, however, is still ardently desired. It will bring them whatever little freedom they can hope for. Until then they must be delivered intact.

We swap jokes and sing silly songs, but after a while the conversation dwindles. I go up to the rooftop with Aziz and Ba Abdullah for some peace and quiet and to snatch a little sleep.

Shortly after 2 a.m. Suraaya comes up to the rooftop to wake us. Downstairs Jamila is getting herself dressed ready to leave. The women have to celebrate her departure. Just as she speaks the chanting and beating of tambourines begins again. We express compliance, but when Suraaya leaves us we turn over for another spell of shut-eye.

But we aren't allowed to sleep for long. About half an hour later we are jolted awake by a sudden explosion of sound from the street below. I shoot up the parapet. A convoy of cars, headlamps flashing and horns blaring, is approaching the house. Behind them, just coming into view at the far end of the street, is a small crowd on foot. At their head is the *aîssawa*, a djellabah-clad band, dancing in time to the beating of tambourines, the blowing of flutes and the energetic sawing of violins. Behind them come Abdeslame and his friends, edging forward with linked arms.

As the band advance, Jamila's friends and sisters rush out of the house to meet them and join in their chanting, providing the ululatory descant that only the women sing. No one seems to bother about disturbing the neighbours. Lights soon shine out from the surrounding houses. Heads bob up on rooftop parapets and figures stand expectantly in open doorways. At last the band enters the house, its powerful rhythm seeming to rock the whole place to its foundations.

Abdeslame leaps upstairs to collect his bride. She is putting the final touches to her last transformation of the day, a fitting long white wedding dress and veil, helped by two of her married women friends. As Abdeslame sits waiting he looks unusually tense and subdued. He cracks his finger joints slowly, one by one.

When Jamila is ready she and Abdeslame link arms and gingerly descend the stairs, followed by the two married women friends, each carrying one of the tall ornamental wedding candles now lit for the first time. Jamila's eyes are shut. She seems in a trance, totally dependent on her husband's support.

Down in the street everyone is bustling about, loading Jamila's suitcases, deciding who is going to ride in the two closed cars and who in the open Peugeot truck with the band.

I cannot help being moved. That silent, white, unseeing figure, being led to the waiting wedding car in the flickering candlelight, seems to have surrendered all self-will. She is no longer Jamila, but distilled into a symbolic representation of the chaste, virgin bride, conscious of shame, conscious of her extreme danger. Because darkness covers shame and protects from danger, it is the element chosen for this final ceremonial of the wedding.

Abdeslame's parents live in a modest flat in Fes Medina. Not in the centuries-old quarter, familiar to camel trains of guided tourists, where the complex maze of narrow, threadlike streets won't admit any transport more motorised than a donkey or a mule, where craftsmen stitch or hammer out and display their traditional crafts in the sanctified shadows of the Karaouine Mosque, or where, farther

from grace, in the lower depths of a Dantean Hell, the tanners, for no
known crime, sweat thigh deep in vats of torrid colour a lifelong
sentence under the burning sun. No, Abdeslame's parents live in a
newer district, equally populous, but less steeped in tradition and
without discernible character, where streets are broader but still
unmetalled, and from where many heads of families still depart,
legally or illegally, for menial jobs in the industrial cities of Europe,
better paid than any they can find at home.

We drive in exuberant convoy through the streets of the deserted
city. It's an offence to sound a car horn at night, our driver tells us,
but for a wedding the authorities will turn a blind eye. An occasional
turbaned tramp by the roadside stops and leans on his stick, watching
after us in silent wonder. Otherwise, scarcely anyone is about. It feels
as though we are the only wedding party in the world.

We spill out of the cars at the end of the long narrow street where
Abdeslame lives. All the windows of his parents' top floor flat are
ablaze with light. Everywhere else, the shops, the houses in the
neighbouring streets are shut up and dark. The candles are relit and
to the continuing sound of the band and the dancing of the more
energetic guests, Jamila and Abdeslame are escorted to the entrance
of the building where his mother waits for them with the traditional
welcome of a glass of milk and a plate of dates. We follow them up the
narrow concrete stairway. The family and the bridal couple enter the
flat. The rest of us are directed up to the rooftop.

Up there on the roof the band plays on, a hypnotic, highly charged
rhythm. Karim goes into a state of Sufi-like intoxication and can't
stop dancing. Aziz and Ibrahim try to calm him down, angry and
concerned. One of their young female cousins suddenly cries out in
anguish and bursts into a fit of violent sobbing. *Crise cardiaque*? Or
nervous hysteria? Everyone crowds round. Abdeslame's mother
brings a glass of water.

With these distracting preoccupations no one is quite ready when
the sound everyone has been waiting for erupts from below. The
ululations of the women echo through the building and Suraaya
bursts on to the rooftop triumphantly waving a pair of Jamila's long
white cotton drawers copiously stained with blood. They are
received with jubilation. The band accelerates its tempo. People clap
and chant. The dancing becomes more frenzied. The garment is
tossed from hand to hand. Ecstatically people rub their eyes and faces
with it. It has magic. The joyful clamour drowns the night.

"The girl is respectable. She comes from an honourable family.
Behold the proof!"

"Is very quick tonight," Aziz whispers to me. "Usually it take a long time. With Merriem and Ibrahim it take a long time. But tonight is very quick."

To this I am in no fit state to respond.

After this it is customary for the women guests to visit the matrimonial bedroom and to congratulate the bride. With the greatest reluctance I allow myself to be swept downstairs, but on the threshold of the room I freeze. The high wide bedspread with its freshly embroidered sheets almost fills the tiny room. Jamila lies in it, still wearing her white wedding dress, the veil gone, her hair tousled and on her face an expression that all too clearly indicates pain, shock and exhaustion. How much, I wonder, is such a girl prepared for this? Aziz cannot tell me. Sex is never openly discussed in his family and he doesn't know what the women tell each other.

"Tu ne veux pas entrer? Mais pourquoi pas?"

The women are surprised I won't go in. But I'm a foreigner. We do things differently. I hope they will forget about me in the crush.

Of Abdeslame there is no sign.

"He is with his friends," says Aziz, "relaxing himself."

I'll bet.

Mou Aîcha and Ba Abdullah have not come with us to the Medina. We must, therefore, take back to them the evidence of Jamila's honour. It is carefully folded, placed on a silver tray and covered with a light muslin cloth. At home it will be wept over and borne aloft by her friends and sisters through the still dark and deserted neighbourhood streets, chanting their pride in her purity.

The wedding celebrations last another seven days. The couple spend their honeymoon in that cramped matrimonial bedroom in the already overcrowded flat. Every day Mou Aîcha, accompanied by one or other of Jamila's sisters, will visit, transporting wedding presents, going shopping, buying presents for the new in-laws, each of whom expects one, from a new djellabah for Abdeslame's father to handkerchiefs for his little sisters and nieces. There are continual parties and servings of hot sweet mint tea. Abdeslame looks relaxed and cheerful. Jamila is more subdued. You cannot tell what she is thinking. When we leave after the last party, she suddenly bursts into tears. The following day Abdeslame will return to work in the familiar *artisanat*. She will have to adjust to her new in-laws and adapt to the ways of their household. In three months she will be pregant. Queen for a day. *Sic transit gloria . . .*

Meanwhile her sisters are hoarse. They lose their voices for three days. They regard this as a small, and indeed inevitable, price to pay.

They at least have enjoyed themselves. In lives so circumscribed, with so few distractions, a wedding is a big occasion.

I have been both deeply moved by this rite of passage and utterly appalled. A quarrel with Aziz looms and finally erupts. I find I cannot presume upon his tolerance beyond a certain point.

"You *critique* our customs!" he flares up with uncharacteristic sharpness.

"Of course not," I lie in my teeth. "It's just that in our culture we keep such things hidden. It's of no importance whether a bride is a virgin or not any more."

"But it is *our* custom."

"It's so hard on the women."

"On the men also. You think it is easy for the men?"

"No, but . . ."

"Tell me. Just tell me one thing. How you can tell if a man he is virgin? How you can tell?"

"That's just the point. You can't. But why should it matter for the woman?"

"Listen. You must understand me. In a family very — how you say? — *très evoluée* — OK — very rich, very sophisticated — it not matter so much if a girl she is virgin or not. But in a poor family is different. A poor family they have nothing in the society. They have no money, no position. No one give them respect. But they have their own respect. So their *honneur — tu comprends ce que je veux dire? —* OK — *leur honneur c'est la pureté de leurs jeunes filles.*"

This conversation takes place a few days after the wedding celebrations are over. We are standing near the ruined Tombs of the Merinids, an ancient and once immensely powerful royal dynasty, looking out over the old city of Fes, its white and sand-coloured buildings heaped up in promiscuous profusion over the steep dry hillside. It is a noted viewpoint for tourists. All the coaches draw in here and a luxury hotel has recently been built nearby. This is how I first viewed Fes myself one summer morning when I never expected to return. Here west looks east and confronts Islam. On the main road behind us old men jolt by on mules or donkeys, while the trucks and cars that sweep by at intervals look makeshift and rusty, held together by flimsy but hopeful contrivance. Their angry wheels churn up clouds of dust. People shuffle by in broken footwear. They have none of the purposeful, energetic pace of the western city-dweller, only the measured, weary plodding of the poor. On the slope below us an old woman, her head packaged in knotted head-squares, sits by an old man crowned with a white turban, companionably enfolded in their djellabahs in the shade of a twisted olive tree. Scattered about in apparently random fashion further down are family graves, many encased in stiff rectangles of concrete, all facing Mecca in eternal expectation of resurrection. By the side of the road sprout giant clumps of rigid cactus leaves.

"You know what they are called?" Aziz asks me. "They are called *sabra*. It mean 'sword'. Like the Palestinian refugee camp, you remember?"

It's a long way to come for a love affair, in place, in time, in understanding. Different countries jostle simultaneously. It's also a harsh environment, on men and women equally. Individualism is frowned on and yet many individualists who could settle nowhere else have found a home here. The poverty is grim, but the pace of life does not harass the human spirit. The sun warms rich and poor alike and the dust shows no fine social distinctions either. To the south are the limitless spaces of the desert and at night there are the stars. Its fascination, amid so much that might be calculated to repel, is indefinable. You have to fall under its spell.

Idly, and a shade pruriently, I wonder what will happen to the evidence of Jamila's virtue. Is there a sort of family shrine where such bloodstained garments are permanently lodged?

Aziz is blunt and to the point.

"They will be shown to everyone and then they will be washed."

Ask, as they say, a silly question. Waste not, want not, as a thrifty grandmother of mine used to say.

Both Jamila and Merriem had boys as a result of their respective confinements. But Jamila's was a difficult birth, during which she nearly died. On such mortal precariousness does her value as a wife and mother depend.

Jackie Kay

KAIL AND CALLALOU

you know they passport forms
or even some job applications noo-a-days
well there's nowhere to write
Celtic-Afro-Caribbean
in answer to the origin question
they'd think that a contradiction
how kin ye be both?

Whit is an Afro-Scot anyway?
mibbe she can dance a reel and a salsa
remember Fannie Lou Hamer and Robert Burns
and still see Tam o' Shanter taken with Cutty Sark
— whit do you think of pair meg's tail being pulled off like that?
mibbe they wear kilts and wraps
and know that Ymoja offered yams and fowls
and Corra could prophesize

you wad think that Corra
wad know something aboot Celtc-Afro-Caribbeans
wouldn't you. I mean what is the point
in having goddesses if they
canny tell you a thing or two about thingymigig

I can see you sleekit eyes
all scrunch up
what's she rabbiting on aboot
she's a blether of hell
— do you think there's mony afro-scots in hell
mibbee there we can hae a party.

I'm eating callalou and kail now
tattie scones and pumpkin pie
so many foods I never tasted
mango before I was nineteen
or yam or cocoa root or sugar cane
like I never read Ngugi or Bessie Head
Only Hugh MacDiarmid and Liz Lochhead
(and they werenie even taught in school)
Liz was my teenage hero
OCH MEN and her stop and start rhythm
I hadn't heard of Audre Lorde then.

See me. I can celebrate halloween and hogmony
make a turnip lantern and dook for apples
take a lump of coal and go first footing
(The English don't know how to celebrate either
sometimes I wonner if they've got a sense of humour
och them sassenachs don't even believe in Nessie
I'm telling ye she's for real
my big brother's got a picture. Genuine, no kidding.)

when I was a wean
I knew aboot the Bogie man
the other day my pal was telling me
about a ghost called duppy. Aye.
I'm finding out more and more
another culture another language
I'm no forgetting the roads and the miles though
when someone sings Ae Fond kiss
I can still tremble
or Will Ye go Lassie go
Aye Actually. I'd love to go to Lagos someday
and I'll aye be back again.

Kath Hardie

WAS YOUR MOTHER'S NAME JOCASTA?

Wouldn't you turn off that old television, and put on your coat and come down to the hall to hear Adam Mann reading his poetry, says Mary McCarthy to me.

Ever since her husband poor John McCarthy died three years ago there's no holding Mary McCarthy. She's out at least two nights every week going to classes and concerts and all kinds of tomfoolery, that a farmer's wife nearing seventy has no call to be interested in. Apart from the Farmer's Journal, John had no use for any kind of books at all and what would he want with them.

In my day I could have had the pick of the men of the parish, but I suppose it was not to be. I'm just as well off. I'm my own boss and who could ask for more.

Well, says Mary, are you coming with me?

Is he a real poet, says I, like you have in books and the like, or is he somebody like Eugene Casey. Eugene, as everybody knows, writes a beautiful poem in the Ballynanogue Tribune every time the Ballynanogue Ramblers get into the league. What's more, aren't the poems set to the same lovely tune, Kelly the Boy from Killane, so that all the lads can sing them in the pub afterwards. That is, when the football team does win. No, no, Julia, says she. This fellow Mann has whole books of poems written and sometimes he reads his poems on the wireless. He was even on television. There are some people, says she, who would be ashamed to admit they had never heard of him. Trying to show me up, of course.

Is that all we would be doing for the night, for the whole night, says I, just listening to this fellow. No, no, Julia, says she. He'll tell us all about the poems, and the background to them, and we're to ask him questions and show him how interested we are, and how we appreciate them.

So I put on my coat and hat and went down to the hall with Mary. There were all classes of people there all right, and some I thought from my days at school with them long ago could hardly spell the word poetry.

Your man, the poet was introduced. The clothes were nothing special. Just an old tweed suit. The hair wasn't too long but very badly cut. But oh, the shoes. You should have seen the shoes. Shabby, dirty, really down at heel. God help us, says I to Mary McCarthy, wouldn't you think that he could afford to get himself a right pair of shoes. Julia, says she, if you're a famous poet, it's your mind that's important and not your feet.

Your man then started on to tell us all about the first poem he was going to read, about rivers. I'll be all right there, I thought to myself, because if there's one thing I know about, it's rivers. And I farming here on my own since my father died. There's that river that runs through the land with lovely clear water for the cattle. And in my day, at the school, you learned the rivers of Europe, and indeed of the whole world off by heart. In Russia there was the Vistula, the Oder, the Dnieper and the Don. So I sat down looking forward to hearing about rivers, knowing I'd be in my element.

Well, was I ever more mistaken there because I had no clue, from heaven above what your man was saying. There was no indication where one line finished and the next one began. You know how it is in sermons — you can always tell when they are coming to the end of a sentence by the way the voice changes and they pause for breath. But there was no holding your man. On he went about rivers with no word about irrigation or flooding or anything.

I began to feel real lonesome about my wasted night. I could have sat at my ease near my blazing fire watching television. But then, didn't the poet begin on the rivers of hell, a revelation to me, because I was always taught that the inhabitants of that region had their tongues hanging out, stone mad for even one drop of water. With a massive furnace burning day and night, and no mention whatsoever of any river.

When he finished I clapped as loudly as the rest of them, not wanting to show myself up. Then, that eejit of a son of Kate Finnerty's stood up and asked him if he thought there were any rivers in the mind. Just encouraging him to write more, and sure enough, the poet promised to write a poem about that. They all looked delighted. This one poem, I thought to myself, I'll try and miss, if I'm spared.

"Still Life" was the poet's next offering. By now I was wiser. If I might have originally expected it to be about apples, oranges, a loaf of bread and a pheasant stretched out on a kitchen table, I could now be full sure that it wasn't going to be about that. I rustled myself up in my seat and prepared to listen.

At first I thought my ears were deceiving me. But I listened more attentively. They were not. The language your man was using in his poem was only ferocious. It wasn't fit for any decent man or woman either.

The f's and the b's and the c's were in greater profusion than you'd ever hear at the fair in Ballinasloe. I whispered to Mary McCarthy. I didn't think, says I, that people wrote those kind of words down in books. If people are educated, says she, those words sound much different.

So I held my tongue and listened to what those words were describing. What they were describing were parts of the body that you'd never refer to outside the doctor's surgery. And they were describing functions of the body that would remind you more of taking the mare to the stallion than what I always thought of as being poetry.

I whispered again to Mary McCarthy. I never would have dreamed that that kind of thing was poetry at all, says I. If Eugene Casey used those words in songs about the Ballynanogue Ramblers, says I, I'm sure they'd never print them in the Ballynanogue Tribune. She looked at me and even in her whisper, I could sense the scorn. No, Julia, to make those words sound right you must be famous and it must be written in a book. And she nodded her head in the direction of the front row.

And sure enough, there was the bank manager and his wife, and the doctor and his wife, and her sister the nun, and no more wonder on any of them than if they were listening to the Litany of the Saints.

I must be ignorant, all right, I thought to myself. If I hadn't gone to hear that poet, I would have believed that nobody would dirty a sheet of paper with that class of language.

When your man had finished the poem, there were lots of questions from the audience about it, how they felt it made them aware of looking at life from a new angle, and the like, but not one single word about the language. So I held my peace as well.

He opened another book and looked at us. The theme of my next poem, says he, is the mother. What does a mother mean, says he. There was no answer from anybody there — I suppose it was too easy for them so I spoke up. Well, Sir, says I, you can always tell who your mother is, but you can never be sure about your father.

He gazed at me for a moment, grateful, of course, for some kind of response. And what else does a mother mean, says he, looking at the rest of the audience, that eejit of a son of Kate Finnerty's, who'd been asking all those questions, in particular. Again, they were all silent, so

I stood up there and then and said, what else would you think of
when you think of mother but this lovely song and I'll just sing a
verse now, so I sang —

> Sure I love the dear silver that shines in your hair
> And the brow that's all furrowed and wrinkled with care,
> I kiss the dear fingers so toilworn for me
> Oh, God bless you and keep you, Mother Machree,
> Oh, God bless you and keep you, Mother Machree.

They all clapped and cheered — sure everybody knew I was a great
singer.

But Mary McCarthy was only fit to be tied. Will you shut up, says
she. You're making an awful eejit of yourself before the whole hall.

With a determined shake of his head, the poet started to read his
poem about mothers and compared to this one, the other two were as
clear as daylight. There was neither shape nor make to it. Every now
and then, he'd yell out, Jocasta, Jocasta. The whole thing could have
been in Greek for all I understood it.

When he came to the end of the poem, they all applauded. I
wondered privately what great gift of understanding had been given
to Mary McCarthy and the like that had been denied to me. Again he
invited questions but they all sang dumb.

Excuse me, Sir, says I, but was your mother's name Jocasta?

Good heavens, no, he says.

Who's Jocasta, so, says I.

She's the mother of Oedipus, he says, in that great tragedy . . .

What tragedy, Sir, says I, that's the first I've heard of it — where
did this happen?

In Greece, in a play, a long time ago . . .

Mary McCarthy was nudging me and whispering at me to shut up
but I just ignored her. If I had spent my whole evening listening to
your man I might as well find out what he was on about.

What was the tragedy, Sir?

Well, this Oedipus married his mother — by mistake, says the poet
calm as you like. He went on, in my poem you could say . . .

I cut him short. I don't know what to say, says I, only this, the lads
here in Ballynanogue aren't too smart but there's none of them would
go off and marry their mothers by mistake. Will you stop pestering
the man, says Mary McCarthy, to me, but I went on.

I only hope and pray, says I, that your mother isn't alive, to be
making a show of her by calling her after all those old foreign women
who don't even recognise their own sons . . .

At that, Mary McCarthy took me by the arm. Come home says she, before you make an exhibition of yourself. Well, says I, to Mary McCarthy, when we went home, if that's a famous poet, you're welcome to him. I'll stick to Eugene Casey.

THREE POEMS

by *Jenny Robertson*

UNOFFICIAL POETRY READING

Viktor proclaims his poem,
and his room is rich with sound.

Words rattle against unpainted plaster.

Rhythmic Russian rinses darkened windows.

Rhymes shape pictures
in uncensored exhibitions.

Forms unfurl
like forests in spring:
fragile and defiant as birches.

Viktor's voice fades.

The poem sinks down
on unpublished paper,
but the air breathes.

EAST BERLIN

The sun at seven
hammers an unheeded poem
over waste ground
drummed by work-going feet
marshalled from flat to factory producing dust.

Faces phrase a theme:
women's unpainted, anonymous,
men's guarded behind dark lenses,
while boys and girls reflect slogans
curved sickle-like across the morning.

The sun beats on
but the new day's stricter metres
are marked with visas, permits, patient queues.

JOURNEY NEAR THE BORDER. POLAND 1986

Our bus lurched on.
I saw a sign: Treblinka.

The black road ran between frozen fields.
We were thirty kilometres from death.

A hundred thousand ghosts,
thin and white as snowflakes
melted into mud.

Bundled in bulky wrappings,
people pushed out at their destinations.

Ours was an unheated building
where, with repentance and prostrations
the Orthodox began their Lent.

Six weeks later,
instead of Resurrection,
their cries of mercy mingled
with a cloud of radiation.

No feast now for those who fasted.
Ploughed fields spring green with sickness.

Barbed wire shuts nothing out.

Esmee Nelson

ISLE OF MAN

He is Chromium Plate, Esq., C.A., figures make his day; this day looking in his hall mirror, seeing vague other features than the ones he usually sees, that makes him suspect the extra unwanted, compulsive brandy of the night before flowing down his brain.

Pecking the wife he no longer knows, he is down his gravel path, going for a train, his car in overhaul: getting into it with another three; it starting, passing two, three stations, stopping at the fourth — for no one out, or in — minutes passing, talk where there's been none, but no one to say why they stay.

No one waiting any longer, surging out of doors, "his" three with them, leaving he, who sees that officialdom is joining in, while he is going — into himself — out of existence it seems, then back, wanting to RUN.

Seizing a handle that pulls, clears just the space to jerk him through, down — where he sees no one else as he speeds on and on, a train, crossing, meeting him, lurching, clasping him in a fierce embrace against a wall, that so shocks, pleasurably shudders even, that he is silent, hearing snaps of breaking limb and things inside.

Inside for repair and repaired to the point where a leg has been, that is agony, anguish and dope.

As soon as he's able he crutches about before the wife he no longer knows, who fills his locker full of things — and goes when it's done, while he goes — suffering on.

Then he's done with all of it — with her, the whole commercial rot, of which he was important, figuring how to do one out, and in oneself in crafty graft, computers blimping . . . printing him OUT.

Nothing but a micro-chip of that old block, he thinks, fitting the wooden leg to which he's now entitled, which makes him stamp, hard with rage, drop his elocution voice, rasping file, filing with others to try for compensating things with compensating money.

In pubs, taking on loads he finds he now can carry, carrying him through aimless days and places — because his brain no longer wants to work, unlike his sensual, which does (overtime) in "red lights", with one at least who soars him high in exaltation places, and drops in dreadful smash, which momentarily has him remembering the wife that once he knew, the rest of him that went in train embrace.

Forgetting . . . forgetting the road of ice of winter night, falling, cracking — not just the wooden limb, his alter ego.

Aluminium now thought to be a better prop, and once upon it he feels the urge to seize a brush and paint a canvas, "knife" it, as the case may be; cartoon, caricature in newspaper offices. Dark politics inside him, rebel for his own cause. Wicked, scurrilous brilliance, jagged wit, fame that writes his name around the world. All flash and flame, burning victims into libel contemplation.

He gets around in skin-tight cords, three pendants falling from his neck; high caste lovers, élan vitale, wealth splash about.

A meteor hurtling across a heaven . . . that suddenly swerves too low. He's in a crater that doesn't show because it's deep inside himself . . . hollow — and he can't get out.

The aluminium that seemed a precious metal feels incinerated too. He wants rid of it, the canvases . . . Slashes, flails about him in a frenzy, destroying himself, enjoying, exulting in the laceration.

"Out of a limb," he shrieks, but not for long: inside — in psychiatry, and quiet — in a ward, getting fitted with the only thing that now will do — plastic partner for his leg.

Into a plastic shell as well, going synthetic to everything and everyone he meets . . . unto the very one he knows would understand could he get out the truth, because she is the same as he — "unreal" outside, raw, wounded underneath, both legs her own, though one not quite the other.

He tries, she too, but it comes out wrong. Can he, can she stand the strain of a relationship, although they would assure each other they would understand if at any time the one or other should seem to be alive and well, then suddenly drop — "dead". No striving after words that would not spontaneously come . . . that silence would be golden . . .

And so he hides himself away in little but voyeuring, looking at her — through a window, forcing himself out now and then, for he supposes he must go on living, buying things to stave off death, "glibbing" away to anyone he knows — *if* it is in her vicinity . . . how he's enjoying his retirement . . .

She too — in his, but with extra strength to cancel all this out she tries to push to him . . . and feels him grasping . . . gasping as he slithers to the ground — beside a mirror, in which there's time to face the faces that he's been, he first saw the morning after the last night of C.A. life. The last leg of the journey stretched before him . . . that is dissolving . . . trickling away . . .

Esmee Nelson

QUARTET? IN E MAJOR

She Dutch, wartime German slave, practising precariously in a place condemned to die at any moment — of old age, innards proceeding outwards through a grey, thinned skin. Doctoring hands make it fall about at times, debris confused. Cuts sellotaped.

Her instrument's a sewing machine she moves around as death comes closer, my compositions in front of her, me turning the pages of notes that make her quaver and crotchet, for they are wild, wayward things no one else has heard, she instrumental, to blame, lifting me off the peg years ago.

We play together well, crashing in dissonance, me going too far up the scale, off it altogether . . . till she sees how right I am to use way-out chords, chromatic zig-zags, strings that are a final movement of a polyester piece. Point, counterpoint, atonal as Schönberg; tortuous rhythms, twisting, enveloping me, so that I am and not — not at all — without her.

At her side I place someone — on the black notes, found sitting time after time in an hotel at a solitary table, a bottle steeped in ice at her side, four short, mixed, wicked fluids in front of her, she drinking, replacing, withdrawing the one from the ice, thin, black as her skin . . . like playing a flute where I sit, before setting it down with the rest.

But for these movements there's still, stillest life, mute as that "flute", hair polished dome above her silent face, that's nothing but its features.

Hours in my going and coming, seeing at last her go — straight — down the stairs, as if water had been in her glasses.

Was she called to play in some dreadful orchestra of men with an alcohol injection that would not wear off until the night had.

For at one a.m. — or thereabouts — one day we simultaneously reached our doors next door, looking — away.

And later on pent-up alcohol gushed words I didn't know, yet splashed about my room, inundating meaning, until I knew what she was saying — that I was right about the wreck that never showed, invisible to me in previous silent nights as we'd lain side by side.

We simultaneously emerged — and because she now knew I knew — we looked — but not away.

And that is how she is an instrument in my quartet? today.

I've a one-handed player on typewriter keys, hemiplegic — falling over cliff to rescue borrowed book, rising, walking away, sitting down — and down flat for months, locked, trying key after key, some turning, turning back, forcing — till her voice got through — shambling in different language, that translated rage, helpless internal rampage, that in the end did move one side, leaving the other helpless.

Words at last became what most could understand, though some could not sometimes, for she had dropped levels in the silence, seen things that would not do for them, dangerous, "unfitting", removing props, withdrawing drugs that had seemed safe, now side to side affecting — uncomfortable fate in the balance.

It was then she began composing — left-handed, trembling manuscripts, that circulated in steadier hands, that had come by advertisement, giving crits., sending scores galore of what they didn't like, with pieces of their own, notes high and low — crescendo . . . dreadful cacophony . . . till someone sorted and duplicated, while she who had started it all found an assistant conductor, and now had me a soloist beyond relief — on my Japanese SILVER REED.

She existential, knowing she can't command, tool of Someone . . . helpless . . . yet fighting to win and pull herself together in extensor-flexor battles to free imprisoned muscles in so-and-so's techniques, leading the band—one-handed—playing with words that seared pages, blazed some away; marrying the assistant conductor, duetting ten years, gathering our various voices into quires, that travelled, oratorioed triumphantly Art Centres, libraries and universities the world over, I still soloist, going my wayward, discording, recording noises — off.

Home — she rising one morning, dropping — dead; we stopping — because the A.C. could not start — without her. . . .

Our positions have reversed now. She plays for *me*..

There is one across the way from where I stay, who I feel would like to join, for there's *something* instrumental somewhere — unseen — and yet I know it's there . . . that he would like to play . . . coming to his barren window . . . looking if I'm at mine, which is not. Or at my door with other people.

He's alone there — and we meet on the street, on opposite sides, me looking over, he at the road.

Just once on same bus, getting off the same stop, we are close and apart as we possibly can be, he hurtling distance between us, me crossing — in time to see the difficulty he has with his key.

Then suddenly his window not barren any more, plants like mine from end to end, his leitmotiv, *he* now unseen — a signal perhaps — that we match, I would see it a symbol and clue to the other "instrument" he plays off-key, off stage, I hear, though barely audible, lost chords — can't stretch the distance.

Thus I'm straining, getting nothing more — until at that same bus stop one night, my back turned, he stamps past, saying something harsh, strange, masochistic? to two he knows. "That's more than you usually get from Steele," says one, which makes me wonder if the surplus has been for me, to tell me what he is, to test my performance in his *steel* band, sharp, agonised, ugly can't note?

I pass, reappear again and again, but he does not. Perhaps his 'phone — unlisted — ringing twice thereafter within half an hour, silent when I answer, is the pass key that I want.

My recorder is where he can see it. Am I to take it that those two close plants, one tall, one small I now see upon his sill, the others tactfully withdrawing, are putting something on it — duet of he — and possibly she?

Can he range beyond this fantasia on a theme, come out, make the crossing, concerto at my side, hammer klavier, tremble clef . . . appassionata sonata . . .?

I have his name — and a new, mysterious glitter at his window, reflecting? Unsatisfactorily, for it moves upstairs. And when I look about me in *my* room upstairs and opposite, I see that I am gazing in a mirror a hand, not mine has placed . . . reflecting.

What *are* we playing now?

Elizabeth Burns

FOR MARIA SIBILLA MERIAN
WHO WAS NOT BELIEVED

She did a painting for her book,
published in 1705,
of a spider eating a bird.

No one believed it possible,
said it was only a figment
of her wild artist's imagination.

There is no spider powerful
enough to eat a bird, they said,
and besides, they would not want to:

spiders are content in their webs
with the occasional fly, and
their daily spinning and weaving

as nature intended for them.
They do not venture out,
raid cosy nests and eat the birds.

The painting was forgotten
until, a hundred and fifty
years later, a man, exploring

the Amazon, saw with his own
eyes a hummingbird dragged from its
nest and eaten by a spider.

Then, shocked at the unexpected way
in which gentle nature had
revealed herself, men ate their words.

Janette Walkinshaw

THE TIME MY FRIEND MABEL
BECAME AN ANCHORITE

When my friend Mabel decided to be an anchorite, her husband said it was all right by him as long as she paid the £1.37 out of the housekeeping and did she realise she would have to give up the drink. She said the second bit was right enough though that was maybe a simplified way of putting it, but she was damned if she could see where the £1.37 came in.

It turned out that Phil thought an anchorite was the same as a rechabite and his knowledge of them was confined to his Uncle Archie who paid into it for years and got quite a lot of sickness benefit back. The family said it wasn't right since it was the alcohol made Uncle Archie sick in the first place, but even his best friend couldn't accuse him of having indulged after he joined.

Anyway, I was telling you about Mabel and how she took to religion. Phil telephoned me and when I went round I found Mabel sitting there, looking out of the window with her housework not done or anything. That's not like her so I asked if she was feeling ill, and she said no, she had decided to renounce the world, that was all. She showed me a book she'd been reading and it was all about saints and martyrs, and there were these anchorites who shut themselves up in a cell and never saw a human being ever again. I've decided that's what I've been looking for, she said. Well, I tried to be as patient with her as I could. After all, when I look at a cookery book it doesn't make me want to be a fish. There's no such thing as a twentieth century anchorite, I said. Yes there is, she said, and I'm it. I've had enough of people. I'm going to spend the rest of my life in total solitude and silence, contemplating the infinite. I said was she going into a convent and she said no, the spare bedroom. I thought about this for a while and then said in that case could I have her long blue dress with the silver sleeves and sequins down the front. It would need taking in at the waist but luckily she's the same height as me.

Phil wanted to send for the doctor or the social work department but I thought the doctor would prescribe tranquillisers and in my opinion she looked too tranquil already. Anyway, she's always been an independent person and she wouldn't like other people knowing her business. Poor Phil. I found she hadn't made him anything to eat, so I cooked him a nice cheese omelette which I always find very acceptable in emergencies, and he enjoyed it and felt much better. He had a bowling match on so he went away and I went up to the spare bedroom to have a serious talk with Mabel.

I mean, it was obvious what the trouble was. A lot of people want single beds by the time they reach Mabel's age and you don't have to make such a big thing about it. I told her this, through the keyhole, for she had locked the door, but she said I was mistaken, it was nothing to do with that. She just wanted nothing more to do with people. She had never liked them. The rest of her life would be spent the way she wanted it, in seclusion, and we could leave her food on the landing.

Well of course we thought she'd get over it in a day or two but she didn't. Phil thought if we didn't give her any food she would soon be hungry and come out so we tried that, but Mabel was carrying quite a bit of spare weight. She always has been very self-indulgent as this whole business shows, and it would have done her no harm to go hungry for a while. But of course the people who came to see her brought food, sometimes just an apple or a piece of cake, sometimes a boeuf en croute with asparagus, but it was enough to keep her going.

You see, word got round and people started coming. I don't know what they expected to find, or what they expected to get out of it. They sat on the landing waiting for Mabel to speak which she hardly ever did, but that didn't worry them. They would tell her their problems through the door, and sometimes she answered them and sometimes she didn't but either way they seemed quite happy.

It was nice for Phil to have company. He took the whole thing quite well, I thought. You know me, he said, Phil for philosophical. It's one of his jokes. Many a grand night we used to have at the bowling club. He was the life and soul of the party. Mabel sometimes said she wished he would get some new jokes, but then she never was one for parties, and sometimes tended to be a bit of a wet blanket after midnight, but the rest of us thought he was a laugh. We used to shout out the punchline before he came to it. It was great fun. Anyway, he was being very philosophical about Mabel's defection and I did what I could by taking his socks home to darn.

Some Americans stopped off on their way to India. They were very interesting and not at all what you would expect by looking at them, but then they are a nation of extremes, aren't they. It was a bit of a nuisance for Phil to find nothing but goat's milk and dandelion root in the fridge when he was hungry. They sat in a circle round the house chanting, a low moaning sound. It was creepy till you got used to it. In fact you missed it when they stopped. They didn't often stop for they used to moan in relays and it was only when the moon and stars were in a certain conjunction they would stop for five minutes every hour. One of them explained it to me. It was quite exhilarating. You could hear them all the way to the by-pass.

Then there was Mr Smith from down the road. To tell you the truth I don't have much patience for people who have hobbies that make them miserable, but you have to feel sorry for Mr Smith. His spare time was spent phoning up women and breathing heavily. Of course they hung up on him immediately and it made him very frustrated. He came to see Mabel and breathed at her through the keyhole for hours and hours, and went away a happy man. He said it changed his life having a woman listen to him without interruption. He had never believed it possible. He came back several times, but he's on shift work and couldn't always manage.

The People's March for Jobs made a detour to see Mabel and stayed for a while. Their leaders stood below her window to address the crowds. Personally, I think it was mean of her not to speak to them. She'd had plenty of time to contemplate the world's problems, and come up with an answer. If she had she kept it to herself.

I was interviewed by News at Ten standing under Mabel's window. I had my hair done specially and wore my green wool suit. I said it was a good thing having an anchorite in the middle of a housing scheme, for it made everybody feel more uplifted. I said the government ought to sponsor a Nun-in-Residence in every town and do away with the National Health Service. I said what's more the vandals weren't getting peace with all the people about and went somewhere else, so it was an answer to the vandalism problem as well. I was on just before the adverts and a friend took a video so I can show it to anyone who missed it.

A psychologist from the university came. He sat on the landing and asked Mabel a lot of questions about her dreams and the change of life. Of course, she didn't answer but he just sat there repeating his questions over and over again through the door. He was a persistent man, and reminded me in many ways of my late husband. We could hear Mabel humming to herself, and this made the psychologist very excited. Since she didn't answer him he started asking the people in the queue about their menstrual problems. Oh, we had some lively discussions there on the landing, I can tell you.

Poor Phil was getting a bit fed up by this time. I found him one day in the kitchen very disconsolate. The people from the women's magazine who wanted to do Mabel's life story had made an awful mess of the garden with the elevating platform they borrowed from the motorway lighting men to reach Mabel's window. Not that it did them any good for she just drew the curtains and refused to speak to them though they sat outside her window for days, but one of the wheels of the machine went over Phil's prizewinning marrow. At least it would have been prizewinning if it had survived to see the flower show. It turned out as well that all his winter jerseys were kept in the spare room and Mabel wouldn't let him in. With the weather turning a bit colder he was needing them for the bowling. That's another thing, he said. You can't get a decent game any more for everybody wanting to talk about Mabel. I comforted him for a while, and said it was my opinion that nobody could stand their own company for so long and she would soon come out.

Of course, it was inevitable that someone in higher authority would start to take an interest, so that when we saw the Royal helicopter hovering over the house I wasn't a bit surprised. I'm very sensitive to these things and I knew it was just a matter of time before Mabel received official recognition.

Well, the helicopter was hovering and looking for a place to land, and taking a while about it, for I suppose he was more used to the lawns at Buckingham Palace and the gardens round here are very small. Everybody rushed out of the house to watch him.

Except Phil. He grabbed my arm and dragged me upstairs!

But he only wanted him and me to talk to Mabel without all the people around. He pleaded with her through the door till I got fed up and I could hear the helicopter had landed, so I used my credit card to spring the lock, for it opens all doors.

And we went into the room. And she wasn't there. I was quite speechless.

Her blue dress was hanging on the wardrobe with a note pinned to it. It was addressed to Phil so I read it out to him. *Dear Phil I can't bear it. I have gone to Novaya Zemlya. Your winter woollies are in the second drawer on the right. Mabel.*

Well, I did the only thing possible in the circumstances. I mean, what would you have done? Everybody was coming, so I pushed Phil out of the room, and closed the door at our back. We waited on the landing to give the appropriate welcome.

The rest is history.

Everybody thinks Mabel's still there. It would be a shame to disillusion them, for it makes them so happy. Besides Phil's doing awfully well with the collecting boxes, and my cream teas at £2 a time have become a legend. On the other hand, I'd quite like a holiday, but I daren't leave Mabel unattended.

Still, I'm glad she left me her blue dress. It fits me beautifully, after I took it in at the waist, of course.

NOTES ON CONTRIBUTORS

VIVIEN ADAM was born in Aberdeenshire and now lives on the Isle of Bute. After university she had a variety of jobs and is now on the enterprise allowance scheme as a writer. She is married with no children, but has "a desire to give birth to a bestseller!". Her stories have appeared in various women's magazines under a pseudonym, and she has also published some poetry.

WENDY BARR was brought up in Northern Ireland and, after living in London, Israel and California, has now settled in Stirling. *Mystery at Ivy Manor* is her first publication.

HELEN MACKENZIE BELL was brought up in Roseneath, Dunbartonshire, and went to university in Edinburgh. She now lives and works as a teacher in London. *Sleeping Alone* is her first publication.

SHEENA BLACKHALL is an Aberdonian. Her short stories have appeared in many magazines and journals including *Edinburgh Review* and the first volume of *Original Prints*. She is currently compiling a collection of her short stories in Scots. Her poems too have been published widely, and she has to her credit two volumes, *The Cyard's Kist* and *The Spik o' the Lan'* (Rainbow Publishing). Her third collection of poems, *Hame-Drauchtit*, is due out in October.

ELIZABETH BURNS lives in Edinburgh, where she works as a bookseller. She is also involved in women's writing workshops and with Stramullion, the Scottish women's publishing house.

CHRISTINE CHERRY was born in Birmingham, but has lived in Scotland since 1975. She works as an adult educator and Gestalt psychotherapist and has published work on women's education, training and counselling. Her poems have appeared in *Hens in the Hay* (Stramullion) and *Voices of Dissent* (Clydeside Press), and her article "Poetry — Who Cares?" is included in *In Other Words: An Anthology of Feminist Writing* (Hutchinson).

MAREE DEELEY was born in Aberdeen and now lives in Dunblane. Having been heavily involved with Stirling Writers' Workshop, she is now concentrating more on her own writing, and this year won the Scottish National Open Competition. She is currently working on a first novel, as well as working full time.

IRIS DOYLE studied at the Reid Kerr College and the Glasgow School of Art before moving north to Caithness, where she now helps run two thriving writers' workshops. She has a story in the first volume of *Original Prints*, and is currently working on a collection of stories.

JANICE GALLOWAY was born in Ayrshire and has lived there ever since, "despite three major escape attempts". Now working as an English teacher, she has only been writing seriously for a year but has already published stories in *Edinburgh Review* and the Women's Press "Livewire" series, and poetry in *Aurora*.

SUE GUTTERIDGE trained as a sociologist and has worked in a variety of areas including adult education. Her book, *The Imprisonment of Women* (co-authored with Rebecca and Russell Dobash) was published in 1986 by Basil Blackwell. She has four children, ranging in age from four to twenty-two.

KATH HARDIE was born in London of Irish parents but grew up in Ballylongford, County Kerry, in the south of Ireland. She was educated at University College, Galway, and has worked in Ireland, Nigeria, England and Zambia. Married with a son and a daughter, she has lived and taught in Central Scotland since 1975. Since then she has travelled with her forestry consultant husband in countries as diverse as Iran, Ghana and Greece.

JACKIE KAY was born in Edinburgh and brought up in Glasgow. She studied English at Stirling University and now lives in London. Her work has been featured in *A Dangerous Knowing: Four Black Women Poets*.

HELEN LAMB studied at Glasgow University and now lives in Dunblane with her three children. She is a recent recipient of a Stirling District Arts Council grant. *The Witch* and *Pointed Toes* are her first published stories.

CHRISTINE McCAMMOND has published her poetry in *Words, Women Write From Life, Images* and the *Glasgow Magazine*. In 1985 her poem, "A Flower for Winter" (published here), won the Paisley Writers' Poetry Competition. She is married and has a son and a grandson.

LINDA McCANN worked for several years before beginning her current studies at Glasgow University. Her story *The Golfer* was published in the first volume of *Original Prints*.

ROSEMARY MACKAY is an Aberdonian writer. An arts graduate, she has retired from schoolteaching twice. She began writing stories several years ago and has had *Lunch* published in the first volume of *Original Prints*.

ELSIE McKAY comes from Fife, but now lives in Edinburgh. Her poetry has been published in various magazines and are collected in *Unravelling Knots* (Outpost Publications).

LINDSAY McKRELL is studying French and Russian at Heriot-Watt University, has just spent a year in France, and is now in Bulgaria.

ANGELA McSEVENEY graduated last year from Edinburgh University and is currently working in a library. Her poems have been published in various magazines, including *Edinburgh Review, London Magazine, Chapman, The Echo Room, Ambit* and *Verse*.

JANE MORRIS was born in Birmingham, studied English and medicine at Cambridge, and is now training as a psychiatrist in Edinburgh, where she lives with her husband and daughter. One of her short stories appeared in the first volume of *Original Prints*; she has also published sonnets and contributed to women's magazines. She was medical columnist for *Cosmopolitan* for two years.

WILMA MURRAY is a lecturer in the Geography Department of Aberdeen College of Education. She started writing seriously about five years ago, since when her stories have been published in *Scottish Review*, *New Edinburgh Review*, *Scotsman Magazine*, *Glasgow Magazine*, *The New Writer*, *New Writing Scotland* and the first volume of *Original Prints*.

ESMÉE NELSON lives in Giffnock and is interested in all the arts, from architecture to astronomy. She has published stories in various magazines, including *Edinburgh Review*, *The Accountant* and *The Birmingham Post*.

BRIDGET O'HARE divides her time between Glasgow and Tobermory, Isle of Mull. She writes poems and short stories.

JOY PITMAN has worked as a teacher of English and creative writing, an archivist, a mother, a publisher (she is a founder member of Stramullion) and administrator. Her poems have appeared in *Hens in the Hay* (Stramullion), *Spare Rib*, *Radical Scotland* and *Chapman*, and she had a story in the first volume of *Original Prints*.

CHRISTINE QUARRELL was born and lives in Glasgow. She was introduced to the Women's Movement seven years ago and now describes her life BF and AF (where "F" is Feminism). She finds writing a way to "work through and record much pain and love and pleasure".

JENNY ROBERTSON has worked as a social worker in Glasgow and Liverpool. She also worked one summer in Schleswig-Holstein with victims of concentration camps and ex-slave labourers, which involved her then in the study of Polish language and literature and a year at the University of Warsaw. She has published ten children's books, both novels and short stories as well as several retellings of Bible stories, including the Ladybird Bible Books and a regular series for Scottish Television. She has been involved in radio broadcasts, and her play, *Aida of Leningrad*, was performed twice in Edinburgh in 1986. She has lived in Edinburgh since 1978. Her poems have been published in various magazines and a collection, *Beyond the Border*, will appear in the *Chapman* New Writing Series.

DILYS ROSE was brought up in Glasgow and now lives in Edinburgh with the writer Brian McCabe and their daughter, Sophie. She has published her work in many magazines including *Lines Review, Chapman, Cencrastus, New Writing Scotland, Scottish Short Stories* and the first volume of *Original Prints*. She was awarded a Scottish Arts Council Bursary in 1985, and is currently involved in the Writers in Schools scheme.

JENNIFER RUSSELL graduated from Glasgow University last year, and is now studying design at Glasgow School of Art. Her story, *The Evil Planets*, was included in the first volume of *Original Prints*.

ALISON SMITH was born and brought up in Inverness, studied English at Aberdeen University and is currently a postgraduate student at Cambridge University. Her writing has been published in *The Scotsman, New Statesman, New Writing Scotland* and *The Sunday Times*. Her play, *Stalemate*, was performed at last year's Edinburgh Festival Fringe.

GILLEAN SOMERVILLE lives in Stirling, but is presently in Morocco. She has recently completed her first novel.

JANE STRUTH lives in Strathaven with her husband, four children and dog. Her story "The Tearoom" appeared in the first volume of *Original Prints*.

JANETTE WALKINSHAW lives on a smallholding in Renfrewshire with her husband and numerous animals. She has had a number of short stories published. "The Time My Friend Mabel Became An Anchorite" was broadcast as a radio play on Radio 4 in November 1986.